Abused

Abused

*A Guide to Recovery
for Adult Survivors of
Emotional/Physical
CHILD ABUSE*

Dee Anna Parrish, MSSW

Station Hill Press

Published by Station Hill Press, Inc., Barrytown, New York 12507.

Design by Susan Quasha.

Distribution by The Talman Company, 150 Fifth Avenue, New York, New York 10011.

Library of Congress Cataloging-in-Publication Data

Parrish, Dee Anna.
    Abused: a guide to recovery for adult survivors of
emotional/physical child abuse / Dee Anna Parrish.
    p. cm.
    Includes bibliographical references.
    ISBN 0-88268-089-7 : $8.95
    1. Adult child abuse victims—Rehabilitation. I Title.
RC569.5.C55P37   1990
616.85'822—dc20   89-26282
                                                             CIP

Manufactured in the United States of America.

Contents

Part Two: Resource Reference Guide

Appendix

Author's Note

Since I began work on this book a few years ago, my life has been truly remarkable. I've had the opportunity to speak to hundreds of people from all walks of life, and I've heard from hundreds more who, like many of you, have had an abusive parent. After hearing so many heartbreaking stories about childhood treatment and the resulting emotional difficulties, I am more convinced than ever that this subject must be presented to as many as will listen. For this reason, I plan to dedicate the remainder of my professional life to that endeavor.

In many ways it has been the most exciting and fulfilling time of my life. It has also been an equally stressful time due to significant traumatic losses in my personal life. I will share those with you in the beginning and at the end of this book.

This book is dedicated to my Mom, who was the best parent she knew how to be. There was never a doubt in my mind that she loved me. She's gone on now, and I miss her. And to my Dad, who feels lost without her, I love you.

To Diana, David, and Mary Carol, my own adult children to whom I was not a perfect parent: I love you too. I wish I'd known then what I know now—how different your lives might have been.

And to parents and their adult children everywhere who are re-evaluating their relationships with each other: good luck!

Acknowledgements

I would like to thank all of the professionals upon whose expert knowledge I have drawn, specifically those who have helped me through the excruciating process of producing this book.

Chris Combs, Dr. Bonnie Gene Ritter, Vicki and Fred Dodd, Dr. Harry Brick, Don Baer, Dr. Bill Irvin, Dr. Jean Tant: these are but a few of the people who encouraged me to see this project through. A very special thanks to my friend, Dr. Fred Fisher, editor of *Adult Survivor Newsletter*.

I owe a special debt to my agent, Lloyd Jones, to my editors, Cathy Lewis and Evan Pritchard, and publishers George Quasha and Susan Quasha.

A special thanks to Lynn Pritchard for the research and inspiration which led to the creation of the chapter, "Digging Into the Past."

I also want to thank Carol Bockes whose help with the word processor "monster" was crucial. Joe Paul Maroof: you have been my ultimate supporter.

Thanks Dear Hearts
"You are the wind beneath my wings."

Dee Anna

The little world of childhood with
its familiar surroundings is a model
of the greater world. The more
intensively the family has stamped
its character upon the child,
the more it will tend to feel
and see its earlier miniature world
again in the bigger world of adult life.
Naturally, this is not a conscious,
intellectual process.

C.G. Jung

Abused

1

A CONCISE HANDBOOK FOR ADULT SURVIVORS OF CHILD ABUSE

I

Prologue

If a part of your life seems to make no sense, yet you can't put the puzzle together because some of the pieces are missing, this book is for you.

If you suspect that the treatment you received as a child has in some way impaired your judgment as an adult—if your current life seems to lack peace—this book is for you. It is also for today's children with the hope that their parents will recognize any abusive childhood treatment in their own past and finally stop the intergenerational cycle of abuse.

Hardly a day passes in which television or a newspaper does not report stories of child abuse which make us cringe with disbelief and horror. But the incidents that we hear about through the media comprise only a small portion of the abusive treatment that actually occurs. Child abuse takes many forms, and there are a great many degrees of each of those. This book is not only about "child abuse" cases which are obvious and blatant—those which can be prosecuted or that require hospitalization—these cases have been effectively discussed and documented for many years.

My primary concern in this book is about some of the more subtle forms of child abuse, which any one of our parents may have been guilty of, not maliciously, but very destructively, all the same.

This book is for the adult who was too harshly disciplined physically or whose parent exhibited sexually inappropriate behavior. It is

3

for those who had to grow up while constantly being put down, ignored or deprived, taken advantage of, or neglected.

I became interested in the effects of child abuse and in the adults who survived it by working with people who themselves were abusers and who were in counseling or psychotherapy because of their behavior.

When I first entered this field as an intern in a battered women's shelter nearly fifteen years ago, I wasn't at all sure that I *wanted* to learn about violence in the family. In fact, when my associates and I were presented with the list of agencies available for our field placements that year, I distinctly remember commenting that my *last* choice would be a battered women's shelter. But graduate students often *are* assigned their last choice for internships, which is of course what happened to me. I was sure that beat up women and poor little displaced children would be a very depressing and dreary population.

But I was wrong. The job was not depressing and I was soon absorbed in my work with the women and their children. It was so fulfilling for me that I even stayed on as a volunteer for several months after my internship was completed.

I don't deny that it is very frustrating for the helping professional when a woman returns to a potentially dangerous or violent situation, but time and time again this is exactly what happens. This reality is the primary source of "burnout" among professionals who work in the field of family violence. However, it is equally fulfilling to observe the ones who have been in crazy, destructive relationships begin the uphill climb toward happy, rewarding lives. The real thrill is to have had a part in making that happen.

No, working with abused women was not depressing, although it seemed that all of the questions I asked about "why the husbands do what they do" went unanswered. The reason, of course, was that the men did not come forward to be interviewed, analyzed, researched, or studied. Most of what professionals knew of them at that time came through the abused partners' bruised mouths. Throughout that year, every program we tried to implement for the abuser was met, as one of my coworkers put it, with "colossal indifference."

But just as battered women began to surface a decade ago, the abusers are beginning to surface now: We are seeing them in the client role for the first time. Certainly there are those who seek help involuntarily because the court has made counseling a condition of their probation or because their wife has made it a condition of reconciliation. However, many enter therapy because they recognize and want to change their inappropriate behavior and to explore the causes of their actions. And while many of my colleagues are repelled and frightened by these men, they are among my favorite clients to work with. Their lives have been unmanageable for as long as they can remember and their recovery is as important to them as to anyone else. They are generally quite anxious to make changes in their lives and in their relationships with others. This kind of motivation makes for very hard workers, and therapy is *very* hard work.

In recent years I've had occasion to work with another population, one that is not easy to love. These are the child abusers; the physical and sexual abusers who are quick to blame their children, their wives, their employers, the community, and the world at large for their actions. The truth is that most of them were victims of child abuse themselves: The children they abuse are the victims of victims.

Mental health professionals have long recognized this "victim of victim" syndrome. The literature nearly always states that "the majority" of abusers were themselves abused as children. However, I propose that the actual numbers are far greater than those who report having been abused. Individuals seem to have some inherent quality that disallows criticism of Mom and Dad. Our social and religious upbringing has exaggerated that notion and makes us reluctant to honestly assess how our treatment by parental figures has affected our current lives. To hear a person deny that he or she was abused and then proceed to describe the brutal, violent, abusive physical or emotional treatment to which they were subjected is not an uncommon occurrence.

"Oh no, I was never abused!" one man told me, but then a chilling look seeped into his eyes as he began to recall the horrors of the past:

> . . . but boy, my dad used to beat the living *SHIT* out of me with his belt, and sometimes he would do it for an hour at a time. And the more I cried, the harder he'd hit. He'd whip me until he got tired and I'd have to stand there and wait while he caught his breath and then he'd start again. And what made it worse was that I had to dread it

all day because when I did anything that my mother didn't like she would say, "You just wait till your dad gets home," and I knew she wouldn't forget to tell him.

He looked almost amused when he said, "You know, I could count on that happening almost every night for I don't know how many years." Then the man quickly qualified all of this with the statement that I have heard from countless others before and since: "but only when I needed it."

But what child needs abusive treatment?

II

What Is Child Abuse?

What is child abuse? Surprisingly enough, people don't seem to know. Most people think that the harsh, rigid, often brutal treatment they received was not *child abuse* just because they didn't have to go to the hospital. People justify the physical abuse they received and that they pass along to their own children in various ways. One of the things we often hear is: "The Bible says if you 'spare the rod you spoil the child.'" I'm not a theologian or a Bible scholar by any means, but some of those who are have explained to me that this phrase is a shepherd's metaphor and that there is virtually no reason for sheep to be hit. On the contrary, the shepherd's rod and staff are protectors, used to guide and comfort the flock. So, to "spare the rod" actually means, to "not provide comfort, guidance, and protection."

When a man I interviewed recently was asked if he was physically abusive, he replied, "Well, I don't break no bones or put out no eyes, but I sure gits after 'em wif my belt." There's probably not a Child Welfare Department in the country who could open a case on this man and his family, for with no broken bones, put-out eyes, burns, bleeding, or internal injuries, the priority for investigation is very low. And, although Child Protective Service Workers know very well that there is a huge gray area between normal parental discipline and abusive physical treatment, the realities of high case loads and low funding prohibit investigation of all but the most extreme cases.

Most parents don't maliciously set about to cause long-term prob-

7

lems for their children. However, in a multitude of cases, emotional damage is the end result. In fact, these parents are probably completely unaware that they are abusively disciplining their children. It is simply the same treatment they received as children, and they react and discipline the same as their parents before them.

An interesting phenomenon which I've observed over the past few years is that parents who received harsh, rigid discipline as children seem to react in one of two ways: Because of the abusive treatment received in childhood, either they are abusive with their own children, or they are adamantly opposed to abusing their own children. We've yet to determine the reason why any one abused parent reacts one way and not the other. It would be interesting to discover the element that makes the difference.

As stated earlier, most types of abuse exist in varying degrees. I think that the varying degree of physical and emotional abuse is self-explanatory. However, one of the issues not often addressed is that there are widely varying degrees of sexual mistreatment. It can range from occasional inappropriate touching, incessant teasing or embarrassing verbal innuendoes, all the way to rape and other atrocities that may continue for years. There's likely to be a high correlation between the degree of abuse and the degree of emotional disturbance that people suffer in adulthood. Most individuals don't recognize the treatment they were subjected to as deviant because it was the norm of their existence, and everyone they knew received the same harsh treatment. That knowledge, unfortunately, does not make destructive treatment any less destructive.

I'm sure there are those who were beaten with a belt as children and feel they are all the better for it. However, this book is written for the adult survivors of child abuse who are definitely not "all the better for it" and who are able to recognize it as the source of their current emotional difficulties.

I'm not suggesting that a parent must never strike a child, although this is the belief of many of today's child development experts. As a parent myself, I realize that such notions may be a little unrealistic and ineffective in the face of sibling chaos or whathaveyou. Often, especially in the case of small children, a swat on the bottom may be the only way to get their attention. But it is not my intention to go into appropriate methods of discipline in this book. There are countless good books on the market about positive parenting. Rather, I want to discuss the long-term effects of inappropriate discipline and other forms of abuse and to present the specific steps one must take in order to resolve the consequences of his or her abusive upbringing.

Parenting is a complex and confusing occupation and the simple fact is that we never find a person who has had a perfect parent or who has been one. The perfect parent would be faultless and there are no faultless people. For one of the most important jobs in the world—parenting—there are no prerequisites. A longtime Child Welfare worker stated it very well when he said, "It's the easiest thing in the world to become a parent, and the hardest thing in the world to *be* one!"

How do we learn to be a parent? By trial and error, usually, with our parents and their parents before them as our only role models. The molding of the next generation of human beings is an important task and perhaps the ultimate responsibility. But too often we muddle through it, leaving in our wake confused adult children who, if they are smart enough, end up in the therapist's office.

**Be the parent who,
as a child,
you'd like to have had.**

III

Self-Test

Most children love their parents, and yet most of us recall incidents that were unpleasant too. After all, whose childhood was ever a bed of roses? What relationship is without its ups and downs? Few if any.

But does this mean we were abused children? To help yourself decide this important question, respond with a yes or a no to the following statements:

SELF-TEST A

_____Yes	_____No	Ours was not an affectionate family.
_____Yes	_____No	I never received physical or verbal affection from my parents and when I tried to initiate it myself, I was ridiculed.
_____Yes	_____No	My parents never loved, respected, or valued me.
_____Yes	_____No	I could never do anything right.
_____Yes	_____No	I was repeatedly told that I was stupid, fat, or ugly.
_____Yes	_____No	My mother was constantly critical about my weight.
_____Yes	_____No	I was never able to live up to my sibling.
_____Yes	_____No	I used to dread the fighting between my parents.

_____Yes _____No   I couldn't have friends over for fear that my dad would be drunken and disorderly.

_____Yes _____No   My mother always said their fighting was because of me.

_____Yes _____No   My parents communicated disapproval by means of sarcasm.

_____Yes _____No   My thoughts and feelings were always discounted, and often ridiculed.

_____Yes _____No   I couldn't talk about my mistakes or disappointments without hearing a lecture or an "I told you so."

_____Yes _____No   I was threatened with supernatural punishment like, "You're going to burn in Hell forever."

_____Yes _____No   My parent whipped me with a weapon (belt, strap, coathanger; anything other than an open hand).

_____Yes _____No   Physical punishment seemed more like vengeance than discipline.

_____Yes _____No   Physical punishment was ritualistic.

_____Yes _____No   I used to have to hide my bruises.

_____Yes _____No   I tried so hard to get attention but got it only when I was bad.

_____Yes _____No   I had no childhood because I had to raise my brothers and sisters.

_____Yes _____No   My mother was such an emotional cripple that I really had to take care of her.

_____Yes _____No   My mother was seductive.

_____Yes _____No   My dad teased me constantly about my body and my sexuality.

_____Yes _____No   My dad was always grabbing or touching my breasts.

_____Yes _____No   My dad barged into the bathroom any time he wanted to. I was not allowed to lock the door.

_____Yes _____No   My dad told filthy jokes to me and my friends and we were all embarrassed.

_____Yes _____No   My dad always wanted me to sit on his lap and I could often feel his erection.

_____Yes _____No   When my dad was drinking he'd kiss me and try to put his tongue in my mouth.

Did you find some of these statements to be true for you?

Some statistics say that up to 98 percent of American families are dysfunctional in some way. This is a startling number, implying that millions of us are not living completely in the present moment but are still locked into the past, still resolving the emotional scars left on us by our parents. But should 98 percent of us be rushing to our therapists? Hopefully not!

If you found from completing the Self Test above that your childhood experience was abusive, and wonder if you should seek the help of a therapist, ask yourself these questions:

SELF-TEST B

_____Yes _____No   Am I always wondering "What's wrong with me?" even when things are okay?

_____Yes _____No   Is my anger inappropriate and nonconstructive?

_____Yes _____No   Is my anger causing me problems?

_____Yes _____No   Am I usually depressed?

_____Yes _____No   Do I generally feel lost and lonely?

_____Yes _____No   Am I drinking too much?

_____Yes _____No   Am I able to keep a job?

_____Yes _____No   Am I abusing my wife/husband/lover?

_____Yes _____No   Am I abusing my children?

_____Yes _____No   Do I tend to get into unhealthy relationships?

_____Yes _____No   Do I tend to sabotage good relationships?

If you are unhappy with the number of YES answers you gave to these questions, maybe you should look into some form of counseling.

Occasionally clients come into my office with other statements such as "My father raped me three times a week for seven years"; "My mother used to lock me in a dark basement for punishment"; "Child Welfare placed me in Foster Care after my dad nearly killed me"; "I grew up in an orphanage and still don't know who my parents were."

These folks don't need a checklist to tell them whether they were abused or not, they know!

IV

What Are the Symptoms of Child Abuse?

Mental health professionals are constantly in the process of identifying symptoms of emotionally disturbed adults. In the past few years we have learned a great deal on this subject from the Adult Children of Alcoholics program. Experts in this field have listed the major issues that need to be resolved between adults and one or both of their parents who were alcohol abusers. However, the behavior problems that plague this group are certainly not unique to them. On the contrary, they are the symptoms common among people who have grown up in any kind of dysfunctional family. Adult children of alcoholics, children of physical and sexual abusers, children of verbal or emotional abusers, and children of parents who abused them through neglect and deprivation are all members of dysfunctional families.

When grown, these children become adults who are faced with the same traumatic life experiences that are encountered by everyone. But for them the difficulties in dealing with these normal experiences are greatly exaggerated and intensified, due to their lack of coping skills.

The following symptoms contribute to this situation and greatly complicate their already complicated lives:

15

1. Low Self-Esteem
2. Inability to Trust
3. Isolationism
4. Feelings of Powerlessness
5. Fearful Consciousness
6. "Bad" Consciousness
7. Hateful Consciousness
8. Denial of Feelings
9. Suppression of Memory
10. Repression of Memory

1. Low Self-Esteem

In my experience as a therapist, I can easily say that 99% of all the adults, adolescents, and children that I have seen over the years suffer from that vague yet all-encompassing affliction we call low self-esteem. Regardless of the visible problem, whether it is depression, relationship dysfunction, eating disorders, or drug abuse, the bottom line is that the person usually has a *zero* self concept.

We know that children who are continually beaten have a very hard time developing a healthy self-esteem. Children who are continually yelled at and criticized have an equally difficult time in this area of development. We also know that this kind of treatment knows no socio-economic boundaries. Ironically, parents who are very high achievers themselves often have children with low self-esteem, because they are often the *most* critical of their children and the most rigid in their expectations of them.

Children want and need three emotional gifts from their parents: their attention, their affection, and their approval.

I wonder how many times you have witnessed this scene: twenty mothers sitting around the swimming pool, sunbathing or visiting with friends, and thirty or forty kids jumping in and out of the water and every single one of them yelling, "Mom, watch me! Mom, look at this! Mo – ther!" In other words, "Mom, please pay attention to me and please tell me that you notice how great, talented, and smart I am." They are asking for the unconditional love and affection that every child deserves and needs in order for his or her self-esteem to develop.

Self-esteem, or its absence, develops in childhood, nurtured by our "significant persons" such as parents, grandparents, siblings, and other caregivers. When self-esteem has not been sufficiently nurtured, then individuals begin adulthood with a deficit. When children have been deprived of parental respect and warmth along with clearly defined boundaries, it is very much more difficult for them to build self-esteem as adults.

Parents withhold, for a variety of reasons, the praise, rewards, compliments, and attention that their children require for building healthy self-esteem.

Single parents may be physically or emotionally unavailable to their children due to the realities of holding two or three jobs, or the pain of the breakup of the marriage. These people love their children but are so caught up in their own suffering and the mending of their own lives that they are genuinely unaware of the suffering of the children.

Many people are unable to demonstrate verbal or physical affection because they say it is foreign to them. They did not receive affection as children and cannot give affection as adults.

Very commonly, parents have the mistaken notion that if they recognize a child's talents and accomplishments, the child may get "a big head." They may even belittle the child's efforts by saying, "It's no more than we expect of you," or even worse, "Stop bragging."

We know that individuals respond much better to rewards and praise than to punishment and criticism. When parents are generous with their praise and affection the child's self-worth is higher. But, if the messages are negative, he or she can draw only one conclusion: they are lacking in worth.

For whatever reason, when the self-esteem building process of childhood is sabotaged, this constitutes abuse. The child grows up feeling incapable, unappreciated, and unloved. The child begins adulthood thinking, "If my parent doesn't love me, I must be unlovable."

2. Inability To Trust

The first developmental task all human beings encounter is the conflict of trust vs. mistrust—Erik Erikson taught us that. (Erikson, 1963) The task begins at birth and is the focus of learning until around one and a half years of age. The task of a child is to learn to trust his or her prime caretaker, usually Mother. According to Erikson, the infant learns that he or she can rely on the sameness and continuity of the care provider, which also teaches that one can trust in oneself and that one is trustworthy.

Faith and trust in others comes from being valued, cared for, and loved. The problem is that the abusive or neglectful mother is usually not the consistent, nurturing parent required for the child to develop trust. Consequently, what the infant learns is to *not* trust. The child learns that he or she cannot trust his or her own reactions, thoughts, feelings, and judgments. When they cry they may get fed or they may get hit, so they never learn to expect consistent nurturing responses.

Often, these babies grow into obnoxious, demanding children and later on into adults who constantly test their parents and others. On an unconscious level they are asking people to tolerate their demands and to show unconditional love so that full trust can finally exist. When it does not happen, then their worst fears are confirmed: "Just as I thought—you really can't trust anyone."

Since a relative degree of trust is basic to human relationships, the inability to trust makes healthy friendships and love relationships almost impossible. This lack of trust may be the basis for most of the other problems these adult survivors of child abuse face.

3. Isolationism

Due to the lack of trust, adult survivors of child abuse nearly always experience a sense of isolation and often say that they have never really "belonged"; they have always felt on the fringes of any group in which they tried to participate.

At a workshop I attended a few years ago on the subject of adult children of alcoholics, the speaker related that she had only felt comfortable in groups of one and two, which certainly puts limitations on one's life. Actually, the lack of self-esteem, along with the inability to trust, greatly inhibits the development of interaction skills necessary to have a healthy relationship with even one other person.

This stems partly from a child's recognition that theirs is an abnormal family. The embarrassment of this alone is enough to promote a secretiveness and a feeling that they are not as good as other children. This begins a vicious circle in which the more isolated one becomes, the less he or she can trust others, which makes it less likely that friendships will form. This exaggerates the self-conception that "I'm not okay" and leads to further isolation and guarding of self.

One of my clients described the feeling very well:

> When I was with the other kids I always felt like . . . well, like an actor, I guess, trying to be like the others when I really knew that I was different. I still feel that way, and even now I'm "on stage" most of the time.

The paradoxical part of the whole crazy cycle is that because of the lack of closeness with parents, adult survivors of child abuse have particularly strong needs for closeness in their adult lives. Therefore, they often send out messages that suggest a desperation which makes others, especially opposite-sex-others, very reluctant to become involved. The end result of this is an increased feeling of loneliness and isolation.

4. Feelings Of Powerlessness

This acutely crippling feeling comes from a sense of having no control over one's life. Adult survivors of child abuse believe that their success and failure is controlled externally by powerful others. Thus they generally find the decision-making process a very uncomfortable or hopeless one. In order for children to develop independence and control over their own environment they need role models—parents who themselves are in control and independent. This is generally not the case in the abusive family. In an abusive family, the child typically is either not allowed to make decisions at all or is forced to make decisions far beyond what is appropriate for his age. The result is usually a poor ability to make choices. In either case, they learn, incorrectly, that they have little effect over their own environment. Powerlessness is very closely related to fear.

5. Fearful Consciousness

Adult survivors of child abuse have grown up in fear. For some it was the fear of physical or sexual abuse. For others it was the fear of abandonment. But whatever form the abuse took, they grew up with a "fearful consciousness," one that disallows secure feelings and the ability to trust self or others. The more severe the punishment or neglect was, the stronger the fear. This fearful consciousness and the insecurity it breeds causes people to mistrust their own judgment and their own decision-making skills, rendering them ineffective, powerless, or worse, self-destructive. As a consequence, the willingness to take risks, which is required in relationships, business, and the process of maturation, rarely develops or is quite limited in adults abused as children.

Fear and anger are very closely related emotions. In fact fear is often said to be the underlying emotion behind anger. This probably accounts for the high rate of abusers among adult survivors of child abuse. For example, when a man feels powerless and out of control, he may feel frightened and often reacts with anger. His wife and children are often the only less powerful people he knows and are, therefore, the natural recipients of his misplaced rage. From my own work with men who batter their wives, I believe that these men were mistreated in some way by their mothers or female caretakers as children and that they mirror that mean, absent, or neglectful mother, sister, grandmother, or babysitter with women in general and with their partners in particular.

6. "Bad" Consciousness

In a child's world, to be hurt translates into "I'm bad." And whether the hurting is physical, sexual, or emotional, a "bad consciousness" develops.

Parents who abuse their children repeatedly tell them they are "bad," "no good," "ugly," "worthless," and will certainly not amount to anything when they grow up. Children who are told these things over a period of time begin to act in ways that support that belief. Some children protect themselves from hurt by becoming rebellious and hostile and hook up with other "bad" kids. They form gangs so that they can feel safer and a little less "bad" by being part of a group. In lieu of being bad, some children become withdrawn and shy. Again, fear is the underlying emotion involved: fear of being laughed at or further ridiculed.

Many of our assumptions about how to live, what to do, and what to think are formed while we are very young—before we have reasoning skills and before we are able to be selective about what we *do* believe. If we are constantly told that we are bad or stupid, we believe it and we carry that untrue message into our adult lives. It is very difficult to unlearn those kinds of messages. One woman put it very simply, "As a child I learned to read, write, and spell, and I've never forgotten those things." It's the same with negative messages: We don't "just forget" those things.

7. Hateful Consciousness

This is an all-encompassing kind of hatred that literally includes the universe.

Consider this on a familiar level. If you have a particularly heated argument with your spouse in the morning and he or she says very hurtful things and then slams out the door, you are left holding emotions that could stay with you all day. Anyone who crosses you or gets in your way from there on in is likely to get a very snappy little remark.

Imagine, then, a little boy who grows up with hateful, negative statements being hurled at him constantly, perhaps with severe physical treatment added to fuel the growing hatred. Combine this with the abandoned feelings that children develop when they feel unloved, and you can see why he is likely to grow into a man who has a "hateful consciousness." Hurtful things that occur in his adult life just intensify his hatred of almost everything. It is easy to generalize anger and hatred to all things and all people.

8. Denial of Feelings

Most victims of abuse have an incredible ability to "handle" their emotions by closing them out or simply denying that they exist. This is not too surprising, considering that this was their method of tolerating the abusive treatment they received as children. Denial was a defense mechanism that served them well in many situations.

Abused children often have the ability to disassociate or distance themselves from the experience. Disassociation is emotional removal from the situation. In extreme cases, some tell about having been able to "leave their bodies" while the abuse occurred; they describe the incidents as though they watched them from outside. As adults, they refuse to admit that they ever have feelings of anger, fear, guilt, hostility, or resentment.

These feelings do exist, although not on a conscious level. Feelings don't just disappear. If they are not expressed verbally, then they are expressed in other ways. Painful feelings often manifest themselves in depression, phobic disorders, or psychosomatic pain or illness. In other instances, obsessive-compulsive behaviors of some sort result from the blocking of feelings. Some of the more common obsessive-compulsive behaviors include eating disorders, sexual disorders, excessive neatness, alcohol or other drug abuse, compulsive gambling, and addictive relationships.

9. Suppression of Memory

Suppression of memory is a form of denial. It is the partial forgetting of an actual incident that occurred either long ago in childhood, or even recently. In many cases, the victim recalls the experience, but somehow feels that it had no importance whatsoever and doesn't examine it. In other cases, the memory is vague and dream-like and has to be triggered from the subconscious by an unexpected incident such as a story related in group therapy or by a similar incident or place. These half-submerged images can also be accessed by a hypnotherapist, with the consent of the patient. Typically, when the therapist asks the patient, "Were you ever sexually abused by your parent?" the first reaction is, "No. Of course not!" Then later, the memory will come back in the form of a dream or sudden flashback to an earlier time. This awakening can bring with it a certain degree of emotional upheaval and mild shock, but it can be an important step in the healing process of a suppressed survivor of child abuse.

10. Repression of Memory

Repression of memory is a total denial of an event in reality, although it is not "voluntary." In such cases, the subconscious censors, such as the kind that filter out unpleasant or highly charged dreams, go into action to erase all conscious memory of the abusive incident. This is a defense mechanism that initially allows us to go on living after a harrowing experience, but in the long run it prevents complete healing of the subconscious. A therapist can often detect the presence of severe psychic disturbance by the symptoms demonstrated by the client and, if no apparent cause presents itself, may suggest methods of unlocking the unconscious.

Some of the current methods of unblocking the doorway to the unconscious are: Hypnosis (Freud, etc.), Deep Relaxation (Erikson and others), Regression (Freud and Jung), Psychosynthesis Somato-synthesis (Ford), Creative Visualization, imagination, association and art-related therapies (Jung), bodywork (Feldenkreis, Rubenfeld, Rolf-ing, Trager), contemplation, and meditation.

See Chapter 9, "Digging Into The Past," for more information about Suppression and Repression of child abuse memories and how they can be recovered.

V

Caretakers, Self-Destructors, and Other Role-Playing Modes

Since there are no faultless people and, therefore, no perfect parents, it follows that there are few of us who do not fall into the "abused" category. It is for each individual to determine the degree of abuse he or she encountered and whether or not the consequent symptoms are causing problems in their lives.

Adult survivors of child abuse relate to the world and the important people in their lives in a variety of ways that are not always in their own best interests. The following are some of the roles that child abuse survivors play in place of developing healthy relationships:

1. Caretaker
2. Superperson
3. Isolator
4. Jealous One
5. Parentaholic
6. Hothead
7. Self-Medicator
8. Self-Destructor

1. Caretaker

These people may become "rescuers"—always attracting and finding people who are in trouble, so that they can care for them, fix them, or help them. In today's terminology, this person is more commonly known as the "co-dependent." They give to others what they would really like to receive, often enabling the recipient to remain irresponsible. But they give at their own expense and are unable to allow others to give to them. This kind of caretaking generally leads to resentful feelings.

This person is selflessly all-caring, all-giving, and responsible for everyone in their world. With this kind of responsibility-taking, he or she can more successfully demand control, but a kind of control that leads to resentful feelings on the part of the dependent one. No one has the right to make other able-bodied adults dependent. It's not fair to them and tends to make them parasitic. Parasites are primitively simple structures who have no means of locomotion and are unable to survive on their own.

In this role when something goes wrong, it is, of course, the caretaker's fault. If something goes right, they usually chalk it up to good luck.

2. Superperson

Other adult survivors of child abuse feel pressure to outperform the world. They were what is called, in today's terminology, the "Hero Child" as youngsters. They were the responsible ones. As adults, they work harder and longer and feel that they must be perfect. It is their only measure of self-worth. These folks are sometimes called "workaholics."

3. Isolator

Some adult survivors of child abuse are only at ease when they are able to fade into the woodwork. They try very hard to be inconspicuous. This person, in today's terminology, is called "The Lost Child." They ask no questions and make no waves. They often hide themselves by being underweight or overweight or just plain drab. Sometimes they go to the extreme of wearing excessive make-up to hide their real selves. They lack direction and often have trouble finding friends or lovers. The relationships they do develop are likely to be unhealthy, often abusive, almost always with an addictive quality that we call "symbiotic." These people never learned to deal with sadness. By the time they seek treatment, the sadness has developed into full-blown major depression.

4. Jealous One

Many adult survivors of child abuse are extremely and unreasonably jealous, a sign of underlying insecurity. The key word here is *unreasonable*. We all have our sense of security challenged from time to time, but this person goes crazy when his non-provocative wife goes to the grocery store. He often accuses her of sleeping with everyone from his own father to the paperboy. The powerful need in this person to control is so strong that relationships rarely survive. This is one of the most prominent symptoms of the wife beater.

5. Parentaholic

Most adult survivors of child abuse have bad feelings about their parents—either dreading to be with them, or wanting to be with them all of the time, but with no healthy sense of balance. They often try desperately to please them but never quite succeed.

6. Hothead

These people may be very angry, with feelings that lie so close to the surface that they explode at the slightest provocation. They are often negative and hostile and have never learned to cope with or channel their anger. Again, there is the issue of control involved, only this person manifests it in a totally different way; they have an overwhelming need to dictate their lives and the lives of everyone around them. Because they view their abusive past as a time when someone else was in control, they are terrified of being out of control in the present. If they haven't already chased them away, they may be abusing their partners or their children. Their co-workers probably dread seeing them come to work. By the time these victims enter therapy, mere anger has developed into overwhelming rage.

7. Self-medicator

There are also those who "self-medicate"—people who use and abuse food, sex, alcohol or other drugs to dull the pain or the fear.

This can lead to addictions which in turn lead to further problems in their lives.

8. Self-destructor

There are those who are self-abusers or who have suicidal thoughts. If not actively suicidal, they may get themselves into dangerous situations or become extreme risk takers in order to keep their parents worried about them.

When children grow up severely deprived of the parental attention they need, what is the ultimate attention-getter? Of course, self-destruction!

Does any of this sound familiar to you? Obviously, everyone has some of these feelings, and may even act on them once in a while. But if a combination of these feelings and behaviors are present most of the time, the symptoms are probably causing severe problems in your life. If so, I hope you will pay close attention to the "Recovery" portion of this book.

VI

Case Histories

I would like to relate to you some stories from very troubled adult survivors of child abuse and tell you about their patterns of relating to the world. Names, places, and other incidental information have been changed to protect confidentiality, but the experiences are true and are told, for the most part, in the person's own words.

When I interview people for the first time I always ask them to describe for me, in two or three words, the feelings they associate with their childhood. Each case history begins from that point.

Buddy's Story

"The only word I can think of to describe my feelings as a kid is 'lonely.' I was always so lonely. My mother had married my dad during the war when he was stationed near our small town. He left her, though, when I was just a baby, so I never knew him. Mom probably had about a sixth grade education and all she ever wanted to do was hang out in bars. I spent many nights in the back room of those joints, sleeping on beer cases. Those were the good nights, when she would take me with her.

"Most of the time I had to stay home with my grandmother. We lived with her and she supported all of us on her old age pension, if you can imagine that. I remember standing at the door for hours, waiting for my mother to come home, I missed her so much.

"I don't really understand why, as I look back, because she was meaner than a shithouse snake when she was there. Not that she ever hit me or anything like that, so I wasn't what you would call an abused kid, but there were times when I'd have given anything for that kind of attention. What she did was just push me away from her and say that she was sorry I had ever been born.

"Oh yes, I can remember something else—fear. I still remember the sick feeling I'd have when she left. God, I'd cry and scream and my poor old grandmother would have to hold me back so I wouldn't run after her. Once, I was so upset that I knocked grandmother down trying to get away from her, and she broke her hip. She was bedridden for the rest of her life and I've never forgiven myself for that. I doubt if I ever can. Then for several years, when I was left at home with her, it was really me, an eight- or ten-year-old kid taking care of myself and an invalid old lady, sometimes for two or three days at a time.

"After grandmother finally died, when I was twelve, Mom and I were out on our own. She had never worked and wasn't able to get much of a job, so I got a job, too, and together we sort of slid by. But she was gone all the time, and now I was really alone and I was really scared. I was the one who worried about whether we were going to be able to pay the rent and the electric bill and everything else too. There I was, a little old kid, laying down the law to my mother about bringing home her paycheck. It was insane.

"God, the fear! I lived in constant fear. I was afraid the landlord was going to throw us out and I remember lying awake at night, waiting for Mom to come home, trying to think of places we could go when it finally happened. I always pictured us sneaking into someone's garage and hiding there at night and leaving before the people came out to get their car in the morning. I used to worry about how I would wake up in time so we wouldn't get caught.

"It's funny though. When I got a little older, about fourteen or fifteen I guess, she entirely changed. Where in the past she had never had the time of day for me, she suddenly became this doting mother. She hardly let me out of her sight. I remember her coming to where I worked and waiting for me to get off at 10 P.M. as though she thought someone was going to kidnap me. I have to admit I loved it.

"I saw it, at that time, as evidence that she finally cared something about me. I realize now that she was just dependent on me."

Presenting Problem:

As an adult, Buddy was an emotional and physical wreck. He was a practicing alcoholic and an insulin-dependent diabetic—two terrible diseases which are independently very dangerous, although manageable. Together they are a lethal combination. His wife of eight years had left him because of his violence, and he was literally falling apart. "I don't think I can live through this," he said. "And I'm not at all sure that I want to. It's like I'm afraid I'm going to die and afraid that I won't."

His crazy, chaotic upbringing developed in Buddy an almost maniacal need to control. This is really not surprising, given the helplessness he must have experienced as a small boy with an intelligence far superior to his very self-absorbed mother. He had been responsible for his family even though he had no power or authority.

His powerful need for his mother's presence is typical of neglected children. All children have a natural attachment to their parents that has absolutely nothing to do with the quality of parenting they receive. They want and need the attention, affection, and approval of their parents and will go to great lengths to get it; and this is a lifelong process. Although Buddy had held the role of the parental figure in the relationship, his mother was still very much, in her own way, in control of the whole situation. She was certainly not about to relinquish this control when Buddy reached adolescence.

One of the primary tasks of late adolescence is that of separation and individuation. This does not mean that one never again sees his or her parents, but it does mean that one becomes able to function as a whole, independent, autonomous individual. This needs to happen on three levels: physically, emotionally, and financially. But there are those who are unable to accomplish this in adolescence or at any age. In them, there is a symbiosis—a feeling that one is incomplete without another person—that does not allow a normal separation to take place.

This often provokes an extreme anger on an unconscious level. The anger is actually directed at oneself because of the need to become independent and the failure of actually doing it. But it is often the result of having parents who were so domineering and controlling that the young person was simply not allowed to separate.

To some extent this was true in the case of Buddy. Incidently, Buddy was not a nickname but the legal name his mother had given him, almost as if to keep him perpetually a little boy. Later, when he reached adolescence, his mother realized that he was becoming responsible for her, so she attached herself strongly to him. He was so flattered by the long overdue attention from her, which made him feel like a real grown-up, that he perpetuated and enabled her irresponsibility. In this way, Buddy was not allowed to individuate as his mother never dealt with her son as an autonomous individual.

Another reason for non-separation also describes Buddy. This is the child who received nothing from the parent—no guidance, no teaching, no emotional approval. When these individuals are unable to separate, it is because they are still trying, as adults, to get such help from the parent. The less effective the parenting they got, the more desperately they continue to try to get it.

And Buddy did try desperately all through his adulthood. He tried so hard that he allowed his mother to remain as a dependent child for the rest of her life. He did this by taking total responsibility for her, keeping daily contact with her in order to issue instructions on virtually everything that she did, everywhere she went, and even what she ate. If she bought anything without first conferring with Buddy, he always found fault with her judgment. By being responsible for her, he was in complete control.

In the early years of his marriage, his controlling attitude was gratefully accepted by his wife, who was a divorced woman with three small children. It was a relief to her at that time to allow Buddy to make the decisions that had burdened her so very heavily. She saw his preoccupation with his mother as evidence that he was a caring person, but this would later become a major irritant to her in the marriage.

At the time of the marriage, Buddy had a job that allowed him to manage a great many people, fulfilling his need to control. Changes began to occur, however, that caused Buddy's professional and personal life to deteriorate. His wife began to grow stronger professionally and as an individual, and this was a terrible threat to Buddy whose fear of abandonment was understandably tremendous. About that same time, his alcoholism advanced, and he began to lose ground in his own profession. He lost his influential position and began a downward spiral that left him powerless and very depressed.

He began the verbal and emotional abuse of his wife around that time; it was the beginning of the end of the marriage. When the verbal and emotional abuse were ineffective and Buddy was still unable to gain control, he resorted to physical abuse. As is true in most cases of family violence, after the taboo against hitting had been broken, it continued. And over a period of about a year the abuse gradually escalated in frequency and severity.

The final episode of Buddy's marriage occurred after one of Buddy's drunken rages that left his wife with two cracked ribs and a black eye. He had also choked her into unconsciousness. The following day, while he was begging for forgiveness and solemnly promising that it would never happen again, he was served with his divorce papers. He had lost control—of his wife, himself, his alcoholism, his diabetes, and his world.

During the next six months Buddy was hospitalized three times for various medical problems related to his diabetes and aggravated by his drinking. His doctor had warned him for years that he must drink only occasionally and must never drink hard liquor. But Buddy had not been honest with the doctor about how much and what he drank. After the final illness, Buddy's doctor told him that he must stop drinking altogether and that he probably needed some therapy.

Melissa's Story

"I felt different and I felt ugly. My Dad was an alcoholic. At least my mother says he was. He left us when I was four years old, and although I have seen him three or four times in the past sixteen years, I really didn't ever get to know him. I know that we never got any money from him, and my Mom had an awful time trying to support my little brother and me. But she did manage and she even went to school part time for about ten years. She finally got her masters degree in Psychology four or five years ago. It was such a struggle for her, and I'm really proud of her.

"The only thing is that between her job and going to school, my brother and I spent most of our early years with babysitters, and I can tell you that some of those people were not very nice. Mostly, they were just either uninterested in the kids or they had too many to take care of and had no individual time for anyone.

"I don't remember ever being beaten or anything but I grew up feeling like a little orphan kid. There was one woman I had to stay with for quite a while though, whose husband sexually abused me several times. I don't know how many times he did it. I was in kindergarten then but I had to stay with them in the mornings. I hated to go there so much and I would cry every day. Mother used to get so mad at me, and I remember sometimes she'd spank me for throwing such a fit. I never told her why I didn't want to go there. I didn't know why. I really don't remember exactly what he did or said to me, maybe he threatened me if I told—it's funny that I can't remember, but it is sort of a blur.

"Actually, now that I think of it, I don't really remember much about my childhood at all, bad or good. I mean, I know I was a child because I've seen pictures of myself but I don't remember them being taken or any of the events where they were taken. Isn't that sort of strange—not to be able to remember? Do you know that I've still never told my mother about what that old man did to me. I guess I've been afraid she'd feel guilty about it for some reason, and I wouldn't want that to happen because all that she's done was for us.

"She had to work so hard with her job and her school work, and what little time she had at home was spent studying. She rarely had any time for social life, and we were so poor that, even if she'd had any time for us to do anything fun as a family, we didn't have money for things like that. We also didn't have money for things like nice clothes, and I really do think that was hard on me because I could never dress like the other kids and got teased a lot.

"Mother had moved us on the fringe of a very nice neighborhood so we could be in a good school district. I know she thought that was the best thing she could do for us; but the problem was that those kids came from really wealthy families, and I couldn't belong with them if my life depended on it. They all thought I was some kind of freak, and I guess maybe I was. These are things I do remember.

"I always wanted to be popular and be in Girl Scouts and dance lessons like the other girls; but, of course, that would cost too much money, so I never even asked. When I got older and the girls were joining the drill team and the swim team and all those things, I knew I would never be accepted into any of those groups because I was so different.

"I really was an awful misfit. The only kids who would have anything to do with me were the other misfits, so those were the people

I hung around with. As you have probably already guessed, we became the 'druggies,' and I was probably worse than any of the others. I got so hooked that all I lived for was getting high. I dropped out of school, and my mother, whose passion in life was academics, was appalled and furious. It was unbearable at home because we were fighting all the time I was there, so I finally just left.

"I was fifteen years old, out on my own with a very expensive drug habit to support, and the only way I could do that was to be a hooker. And that's what I've been doing for the past five years. But it is not what I want to do anymore. I want to do something about this."

Presenting Problem:

Melissa was a small, quiet, intelligent girl. When she first walked into my office, I thought her to be around thirteen years old and was surprised to learn that she was nearly twenty-one. She had been drug addicted for six years, had been bulimic in the past, and was now a self-mutilator. She called herself a "cutter," for skin cutting was her preferred mode of self-injury.

Self-injury is one of the most difficult of the compulsive behaviors to understand. It seems to contradict two of our most basic instincts—self-preservation and fear of pain. This disorder has been misunderstood by the helping professions until the past few years. Self-injury was considered a suicidal gesture and evidence of suicidal thoughts or fantasies.

In truth, these people are not suicidal and are not crazy. They are obsessive people who are compelled to injure themselves by cutting, hitting, burning with cigarettes or caustic substances, swallowing poisons or small objects, and using various other methods of self-injury. They feel better afterwards, they say, and seem to get some sort of release from the action. And because they are so very out of touch with their feelings—even physical feelings—most claim to feel little or no pain.

What we know about the practitioners of this strange addiction is that they are overwhelmingly female, probably because men are freer to project their aggressions in other ways. They are also usually white, single, and in their late teens or early twenties. Typically, they suffer from eating disorders such as anorexia nervosa or bulimia. Family alcoholism plays a significant role in the development of self-mutilation. And a high percentage have experienced sexual abuse, generally at an early age, probably another factor which explains the high percentage of females who suffer from this disorder.

Sexual abuse by a parent or other authority figure is one of the most damaging things that can happen to a child. It not only destroys the self-esteem but also breaks the chain of trust, often irreparably.

Melissa's inability to remember the abusive incidents does seem strange, but it is not unusual. Sexual abuse is very often so traumatic that the victim simply blocks it from the mind and may be so success- ful at the repression that he or she will have difficulty remembering any incidents of childhood, the pleasant experiences along with the unpleasant ones.

Melissa's therapeutic work began with stopping the injurious be- havior immediately. I required that she sign a new contract each week committing herself to "no cutting." She understood that if she broke her contract, her therapy would be terminated. She was so committed to getting better that the fear of ending our therapeutic relationship was the reinforcer that kept her straight. She received some help with this by becoming involved with the self-help group called SAFE—Self Abuse Finally Ends—which aided in her recovery. She also was put in touch with, and was required to attend, Narcotics Anonymous, going to meetings on a daily basis.

In individual therapy she worked on relaxation techniques and on learning to manage her life. In group therapy, Melissa began to share her past and to learn that it was all right to feel and to express those feelings. As with most abuse victims, this was a major hurdle.

To her surprise, some of the feelings she was able to uncover included anger toward her mother. With the help of the group mem- bers, she began to question, for the first time in her life, why her mother had been so preoccupied with everything else in her life and had not prioritized some time for Melissa. Melissa was even able, in time, to question how her mother had built such a barrier and kept herself so distant that she was unaware of the sexual abuse and therefore failed to protect Melissa from it. She questioned how her mother had failed to recognize Melissa's lack of social skills, and how this had prevented her from having a normal life.

With much coaxing from the group, Melissa looked up the woman babysitter whose husband had abused her. She was ready to confront him and to tell him how he had damaged her life, but the man had died a few years earlier. She had to settle for telling the woman who was supposed to have cared for her. Even though the woman denied the accusation, this was, by far, the most healing step that Melissa took.

Another step that she took was going to her mother and beginning to communicate with her. Because she was so committed to her own emotional growth, she did this after I mentioned it only one time. It was as though she had been waiting for someone to give her permission to do this. If this suggestion had been presented too early in therapy, Melissa would probably have been overwhelmed and more than likely would not have continued therapy.

Melissa was able to tell her mother, in a nonconfronting manner, all that had happened and how it had been for her. Her mother, now working in the field of child development, had learned a great deal about parenting since she herself had been a single parent, and she was open and receptive to the renewal of their relationship. She was emotionally healthy enough to be able to take responsibility for her part of Melissa's very painful childhood. They talked and apologized to each other and cried together over a period of about two months; the healing process was well on its way.

Brian's Story

"I grew up feeling spoiled rotten! I was the center of the world for my mother and my grandmothers and my old-maid aunts. I guess if I'm really going to be honest I could say that I felt a little smothered.

"My parents divorced when I was just a baby, and my mother and I went to live with my grandmother. She was a real strong lady, and I always knew that she was the one in control. My mother was as sweet and loving as my grandmother was loud and gruff. We lived in a small town in southern Nebraska, and Grandmother owned and ran the drug store which was the meeting place and center of the town. Everyone knew her and knew that she was sort of a character, and they all catered to her, about like we did.

"Don't get me wrong, she was a lovable old character and I always knew that she loved me, but it seemed like nobody could ever do anything quite right to suit her. She always found some little something that should have been done differently. Her way was always the right way and everyone, me included, said 'How high?' just as soon as she said 'Jump!' It is still that way, come to think of it.

"My other grandparents, Dad's folks, stayed involved in my life even though Dad moved away and we didn't hear from him very often. My dad's mother had two sisters who also made my life their business. My grandfather was the only male in my life, but he pretty well deferred to my grandmothers and aunts and, of course, to my mother.

"The awful thing was that they all hated each other. When I was with Dad's family they said mean, nasty things about my mother and my grandmother. My mother never said anything bad about anyone, but Grandmother never shut up about how lousy my dad's family was and, of course, what a bastard my dad was for running off and leaving me and my invalid mother. Oh, did I tell you, my mother had polio and was in a wheelchair? She got it when I was a baby, I guess right before my dad left us, and I never saw her walk. But she was pretty active anyway and all my friends loved her because she was a very sweet lady.

"It's funny, though, how I felt when my relatives would criticize each other; I felt like it was me they were talking about, and it hurt my feelings. As I got older, I finally learned to just turn it off or walk away; but when I was little, I thought I had to listen to all that was said. I think I felt responsible for everyone's shortcomings and the need to try and fix them all, even though I knew that I couldn't. I can't remember ever trying to defend anyone from the others, but I just felt badgered.

"My mother died when I was fourteen, and even though my dad's family did come to the funeral, they were very distant and didn't even come back to the house afterward. I remember that really set my grandmother off. She ranted and raved about that forever. She still talks about it to this day, twenty-four years later.

"We had a woman who lived with us, Mrs. Abbott, who was a combination housekeeper-nurse for Mom, before she died, and babysitter for me. She was sort of a tyrant and she was the one who always had to punish me. It was a little strange because, if my mother thought I needed to be punished, since she couldn't do it herself, she would have Mrs. Abbott do it.

"But Mom didn't want to see it happen, so she would have her take me to another part of the house. Mrs. Abbott would always say,

'This hurts me more than it does you, Brian,' but I knew better than that because she was a huge woman and she could hit pretty hard and she would fairly well blister me with a paddle that she kept handy. She would hold me in the air by my arms and whack me so hard that I'd be sure she would break my legs. It really is a wonder that she didn't because I fought her so. But I was a mean little shit and I probably did deserve it. She always said I did."

Presenting Problem:

Brian and his wife, Nan, came for marital counseling. They had been married nearly twenty years, had two teenage daughters, and both stated that they planned to work out their problems. Neither had any thoughts of divorcing, although their relationship had reached a very low point. Nan was a recovering alcoholic with two years sobriety. Brian had engaged in multiple extra-marital affairs for the past fifteen years. Each admitted that their own behavior had contributed to the actions of the other, which was a substantial tool to begin the process of rebuilding the marriage.

Nan's chief complaint was about Brian's violent temper. Typically, although he never struck them, he would lose control and lash out verbally at her and at the girls so viciously that they were terrorized and miserable. They had reached the point years ago that they dreaded seeing him come home. Nan said that Brian had always told her that she was a "self-taught incompetent" and that she had always believed him.

The older daughter had married at age sixteen in order to get away. Nan often commented that Brian would never talk to a man the way he talked to them and that over the years the nasty scenes and ugly words had gradually eroded the relationship until she had little, if any, feelings left. Brian conceded that he would like to conquer his anger, as it was a problem not only at home but in his work world as well.

The therapy began by introducing Brian and Nan to a procedure called "Time Out." This is how it works: When a person is on the verge of losing control, there are always some physical body cues that precede the outburst. In Brian's case his muscles tensed and his heart began to pound—sometimes he actually "saw red."

When the angry person first recognizes the cues, he is to make a

"T" sign, as in athletic activities. The partner is to return the sign. He is then to walk out the door without slamming it and with "no famous last words" from either partner. The "Time Out" sign is a promise to return. It signals this message: I'm going to walk for ten or fifteen minutes to allow my adrenaline to settle down, and then I will be back and we will resolve our differences.

While he walks, he is to think of a technical error that he made during the incident which triggered the rage. For example, he might say, "I'm sorry that I yelled at you," or, "I'm sorry I said you were a bitch." While he is gone, his partner is to do the same, and when he returns, they are to begin with those concessions. Somehow, these apologies seem to de-escalate the anger, and then the couple can allow themselves to solve the problem. If, when he returns, he still feels angry, he must go walking again until he feels ready to resolve the problem. Each person must give a smile or a hug or some other positive gesture. This technique is absolute magic for couples who both are willing to work at it. It allows the abuser to control anger so that he can begin therapy in order to explore the old issues that are at the bottom of his rage.

Brian had breezed through this behavioral portion of the therapy very enthusiastically and, after two or three weeks of anger control, felt like a new man. He was quite pleased and proud of himself and his self-esteem was elevated to an all-time high.

However, he was less than cooperative about entering into discussions about his rather chaotic upbringing and denied that the matriarchal world by which he had been surrounded as a child had been anything less than blissful. The information about his mother's illness and subsequent death had been revealed almost as an aside rather than as the important and traumatic issue that it really was. And, no, he had not felt the least bit of embarrassment as a small boy that his mother was different from the mothers of his friends, nor the least bit of anger when she died and left him prematurely.

He laughed when he described his grandmother's domineering manner and her iron-fisted control of every facet of his life, from infancy to the present. It was with great reluctance that he began to concede that her overbearing intrusion, not only in his boyhood, but into his adult life at age thirty-eight, could possibly be the core of his anger toward women. This was the biggest hurdle, but once he had conceded that it was a possibility, once he had broken that taboo of criticizing a member of his family and recognizing her behavior as less than perfect, he found it easy to continue the process.

He needed little coaxing to reveal the confusion and the anxiety that his whole family had created by verbally attacking each other in his presence. And he was insightful enough to parallel his family's behavior with his own verbal attacks on Nan and the girls.

He needed no coaxing to explore his long-buried feelings that his dad had indeed been a bastard for deserting him and his mother shortly after his mother became ill. It was Brian's considered opinion, with no therapeutic intervention, that his dad had been, in the words of the therapist, "a poor role model," and in the words of Brian, "a bit of a prick."

This all unfolded for Brian over a matter of several weeks. Toward the end of our work together it suddenly occurred to him that Mrs. Abbott, the housekeeper, had been overzealous, if not brutal, with her punishment. "Maybe I was a mean little shit but I don't think any kid needs to be treated like that."

Jenny's Story (Age 13)

"When I was younger, before I started school, I remember feeling very loved. I was an only child, and my parents had waited until they were both set in their careers to even try to have a baby. So by the time I was born I was really something special to them, and they made me feel that way. At least they did until I was in second grade and began having trouble with my schoolwork.

"While I was in first grade someone had come in and given us all IQ tests, and mine had shown that I had above average intelligence. Well, my parents were just thrilled over that and, God, they never let me forget it. When I began making bad grades in arithmetic, they got really mad at me and punished me, and from then on all I can remember feeling was guilty and stupid.

"It was bad enough that I felt stupid at school when I couldn't do the work, but when I got home I'd have to sit for hours with my Daddy trying to explain it to me. He was an attorney, and my mother was an accountant, and they were both real smart and just couldn't believe their daughter was so dumb. He used to say, 'Anyone with your intelligence who can't do this simple stuff—Jennifer, you are just not trying!' But I was trying, I really was, and I couldn't make him believe me. I felt so frustrated! He usually ended up slamming the book closed and slamming the door, leaving me sitting there feeling miserable. Sometimes both my parents would try to work with me, and then they'd both be mad at me and usually mad at each other, and I always ended up in tears.

"Every morning I'd wake up dreading the day at school and dreading coming back home too. Most days I had a stomachache, but, when I told my parents, it just caused trouble between them. My mother would say, 'Well, Honey, maybe she really is sick,' and my daddy would say, 'Liz, she's just working you, and you know she just doesn't want to go to school.' And they would argue about it, so finally I just quit saying anything; but I really did have stomachaches.

"And, oh, the guilt I felt! Daddy would make me feel so bad because he had to give up his evenings to tutor me. He called it tutoring, but I called it badgering. One time, after a parent-teacher conference, my parents gave up a weekend trip they had been planning so that he could stay home and tutor me. Now, besides the badgering, I had to hear about what they had sacrificed just because I was so stubborn. What's funny is that I was doing pretty well in my other school work, I don't know how, because I spent almost no time working on anything but Arithmetic. I always got 'outstanding' in Music and Art, but my parents never said a word about that.

"I managed to pass every year, but by the time I was in fifth grade, my parents were convinced that I was just a rebellious brat, and that was probably true to some extent. I had become very sullen and withdrawn and had no friends.

"Finally, at the end of that year my parents agreed to having me tested and they found that I had a learning disability that affected my ability to understand arithmetic. At first Daddy wouldn't believe it because my IQ still tested very high, but after the school counselor convinced him that a learning disability didn't mean that I was retarded—thank God—he began to listen to her.

"In sixth grade I was in the regular classroom most of the day, but I went to resource class for arithmetic. That's where they teach with different methods, allowing kids with special learning problems to compensate. One thing I learned was that I wasn't the only kid in school with a learning disability and mine was much less severe than some of the others. Of course, the regular kids all called resource the 'dumb class,' but I think I could have lived with that because I'd been such a loner for so long anyway. What hurt me was that my parents seemed to feel that way too. My dad went from the extreme of monitoring my school work on a daily basis to completely ignoring it. When I tried to talk about school, he changed the subject. Now that I think of it, no matter what I tried to talk about, he changed the subject. He didn't seem to be interested in me at all. I'm not sure which extreme was the worse.

"It wasn't like they were mean to me; like they never beat me or abused me or anything like that. But they just gave me the feeling that I didn't quite measure up."

Presenting Problem:

Jenny's mother brought her for counseling the summer after she finished eighth grade because Jenny had become a behavior problem at home. Actually, Jenny had become so withdrawn from her parents that they could not seem to reach her. And although Jenny was doing well in school now, she was extremely hostile and angry toward her parents, and they couldn't understand why.

After Jenny told me what her school years had been like, it was easy to understand her hostility. For several years she had been living in an environment of general disapproval, and those years had certainly taken their toll. She was very angry, but the emotions behind the anger were hurt and fear.

Children look to their parents for support, and they generally get it up until the time that they begin to experience failure, which is the time they need support the very most. And, instead of the support they so desperately need at that crucial time, we, as parents, tend to react in a harsh, judgmental manner, especially if we happen to be academic achievers ourselves. Of course we want our children to do the best they possibly can, but we need to remember that young children want that too. They are still very eager to please and to achieve.

But at least ten to twenty percent of the children in the average school population have problems with their academic work. Some have subnormal intelligence and are unable to function at a normal level. Some have situational or emotional problems that cause their learning difficulty. Still others have average or above-average intelligence but, because of the way their brain or nervous system functions, are unable to learn in conventional ways. This third group consists of children known as "learning disabled," and they represent between three to ten percent of most school populations. Dr. Larry Silver explains this in detail in his book *The Misunderstood Child*. For any parent who has a learning-disabled child, or even suspects the possibility, this book is a "must" to read.

Jenny's parents had been told of Jenny's learning disability, but they saw it as a stigma rather than as the limitation that it was. And they never bothered to learn more about it. Jenny had tried but was unable to succeed in the area her parents felt was important. Instead of focusing on her strengths and abilities, the parents became obsessive about her one weakness. This was frightening to her because the message conveyed to her was, "If you can't succeed in everything, you're unacceptable to us, your parents." And, as discussed earlier, fear is the underlying emotion of anger.

As Jenny and I discussed this, it made sense to her. Consequently, she began to let her guard down and was receptive when I suggested family therapy. I was very careful not to suggest it too soon, as her anger and hostility toward her parents was raging, and at first she could barely tolerate being in the same room with them. But, after I had seen her for about a month, I did suggest it. Jenny seemed to sense that family therapy would eventually need to take place.

It was not easy to persuade Jenny's father that family therapy would be worthwhile. After all, it was Jenny who had the problem. When the family did come in, he sat looking very dutiful, as if to say "Okay, I'm here. Now fix her and then we'll go home."

I began by asking each family member to talk about their feelings back when Jenny was in first grade, before the academic problems became apparent. This took the edge off the first session somewhat, because they were all able to relate positive feelings, which eased their tensions.

As we talked about succeeding school years, the atmosphere was often less than congenial, but all were finally able to share and were surprised at the feelings of the others. I had previously asked Jenny's parents to read Dr. Silver's book. Neither had found the time to do so. This time, before we ended this first family session, I assigned the book as homework, and we ended on a positive note. But I wasn't at all sure they would return the next week. They did, and they had done their homework. Both parents thanked me heartily for forcing them to read about Jenny's learning disability and how to deal with the problems it created. Although, of course, I had not written the book, I was pleased to take the credit for having forced it upon them. They returned for a few more sessions, which were sometimes rather heated, but always ended with hugs.

The important thing in the therapy was for each member of this family to recognize that love had been the motivator of actions, although it had been expressed in a negative manner. Jenny had to forgive her parents, and the family had to learn to communicate with each other. This responsiveness was long overdue.

Emily's Story

"Confusion! I have often thought about what it was like for me growing up, and I can easily say that confusion is the perfect description. And when I do think about the past, my impression is that of walking through a fog—like the words in the song 'Misty, water-colored memories.' I never quite knew what to expect or what was expected of me. Yes, my childhood was very confusing—very strange and very weird!

"Daddy was a physician and a very well-respected person in our small town in Louisiana. We lived in one of those big old antebellum homes like you see in the movies, complete with magnolia trees and a big beautiful veranda, even a winding staircase—I'm not exaggerating. I know it was really as I remember because it is now a museum and I have been back to see it in the past few years. It really is magnificent.

"My brothers were twins, who were inseparable, and were twelve years old when I was born, and my sister was eight. None of them had much to do with me. Actually, they were all away at school most of the time when I was little. I guess I never really knew them well enough to build any kind of close relationship.

"I don't know why, but they were all scared to death of Daddy, and he didn't seem to care much about them either, but he loved me. It was obvious that I was his favorite, and I always knew it. He took me with him everywhere he went, even to the office while he was seeing patients. I remember standing beside him in the front seat of the big Lincoln that he drove. I had anything and everything I wanted, even my very own 'Mammy,' Sophie, who was more like my Mom at that time. I actually don't remember Mamma when I was little, only Daddy—and Sophie.

"It was all like some storybook existence—until I was four years old, which is when the confusion began. Daddy died. It was a heart attack and he was gone instantly, I found out much later. I don't know if I can even describe what it was like for me after that. To begin with, no one explained to me what had happened, where Daddy was, or that he would not be coming home. I remember thinking that someone was going to come and tell me and that Daddy would be home soon, but that never happened.

"And the incredible part is that I never asked, at least not for a long time. I guess there just was no one to ask. Except for Daddy, there had been no one I had ever felt close to, no one I could trust, except maybe Sophie. Eventually, she was the one who told me, very tearfully, that my Daddy was 'dead and gone.' I didn't know what that meant, but I do remember wondering what would happen to me. Since my mother had never been a part of my life, I guess it never occurred to me that she could take care of me. And, in fact, she couldn't take care of me.

"My father had been a scientist and had developed a medicine which was quite successful in the treatment of arthritis. He was a terrible businessman, though, and had invested most of his capital into its production. After his death, we were left with no assets and no income. We were able to stay in the house for a few years, but we had no money to maintain it or to buy some of the things we were used to having. Mother rented out the library to a dance school in an attempt to keep things going, which is the only way we were able to live in the house for as long as we did.

"Mother was either so grief-stricken or maybe she was just mentally unbalanced, but she was the meanest damned woman who ever lived. I know now that she was somewhat mentally unbalanced because, years later, she was institutionalized for a time and then she was better. But I think she had been having a walking nervous breakdown for ten years. God, if only someone had given her a valium back then, how different my life would have been! I just never knew how she was going to react to anything.

"Most days, when I was still five or six years old, I could roam around all over town, and she wouldn't know where I was for hours at a time. Then the next day I might be in big trouble for just walking a block away from the house. 'Big trouble' for me meant spanking, and she usually got pretty carried away with her 'spanking.' One time when I was about seven I went into this little grocery store, and the lady who worked there asked me what I was doing so far from home—I didn't think I was so far from home—and she said, 'I'm going to call your mother.' I know that she was trying to be helpful, but at that time I remember being terrified.

"When Momma got there she had a switch with her and right there in the parking lot, in front of ten or twelve people, she just beat the hell out of me with that thing. I had welts all over my legs for a week and I was so embarrassed. But I think the worst part was, it was so absolutely unjustified and it was so confusing. That is just one example of how erratic she was.

"Another thing, she use to just slap me in the face and I wouldn't even know why she had done it. It seemed like all she did was yell and scream and hit. I hated her, so I just avoided her whenever I could. I became very involved in school activities. I had learned to dance pretty well by standing in the back of the room and watching during the dance classes at the house, so I was able to be in all the programs at school. That was really lucky for me. If it hadn't been for that I probably would have had a much worse time. I always wanted Momma to be proud of me, but she never once came to anything I was in and she was just not impressed with me at all. As long as I could dance, though, that's how I knew that I was O.K. I didn't care that I had to wear tacky old clothes, and I didn't even care that I didn't have any close friends either.

"When I was ten years old we finally lost the house. That began the most traumatic time in my life, not only because we had to live in a run-down dump in the bad part of town, although I have to admit that was quite a shock, going from the sublime to the ridiculous, so to speak. And you know how cruel kids can be. As you might imagine, I had to endure a lot of snickering and sneering about the 'poor little rich girl' and teasing about my riches-to-rags decline. We were dirt poor and I remember many times being so hungry that when food finally came, I was too sick to eat it. But I never told anyone that we had nothing to eat. Momma wouldn't let me.

"But the absolute worst part of it was that I was now alone with my mother. Before, I had been able to find ways to avoid her, but now my brothers and my sister were out on their own and it was just Momma and me, and in that house that was so small I could no longer get away from her. As I remember, she had never been as mean to the other kids as she was to me. I can't tell you how much I hated her for the way she treated me. Now, of course, I feel very guilty about that. After all, she didn't really abuse me and she did the best she was capable of. Do you know that we never talked. By that I mean we never really communicated until I was in my twenties. Our relationship now is much better than it has ever been. Actually, I am the only one of the four who has anything to do with her now and I do try to make life as pleasant for mother as I possibly can. She actually seems to appreciate what I do for her and is even proud of me. I never thought I would see that day."

Presenting Problem:

Emily came to therapy about six months after her second marriage had ended in divorce. She was devastated because she said she had tried her very best to be "exactly what he wanted me to be and he left me anyway."

Her first husband, the father of her two daughters, had been a substance abuser and a womanizer who had made her life miserable for six years. After she divorced him she'd had a difficult time financially, since she received no child support from the girls' father and had to work very hard just to support them. This continued for ten years.

When she met and married her second husband, who was sixteen years her senior and very well off financially, she thought their lives were finally secure and stable, and she was ecstatic. After eighteen months, however, she was taken completely by surprise when he informed her that he wanted a divorce. The only reason he offered was that "it just wasn't working out."

The fact that she was unaware of any problem even as her husband was contemplating divorce is the first clue to the level of the relationship and the quality of communication between the partners. She acknowledged that she was aware of his need for a closer relationship than she had been capable of, and that, if she'd only had the ability, she would certainly have complied. After all, she was trying to be "exactly what he wanted"—not what she really was, but what he wanted her to be. The problem was that she had not been in a close relationship since she was four years old and she simply did not know how to do it.

Emily could easily be classified as a workaholic; if you were to encounter her in her professional world you would be impressed with her friendly, open, outgoing, very personable, self-assured manner. You would be amazed to hear that she felt lonely and unable to relate to people on anything more than a superficial level.

It takes courage to love and to commit oneself. When there are demands and there is a need for sharing and for intimacy, a person who has never learned to trust feels very threatened and very vulnerable. Individuals such as Emily have a tremendous fear of close relationships. They suffer from loneliness and must compensate for their feelings of alienation and isolation by being nurturing and friendly to virtual strangers. They often feel the responsibility for making everyone feel welcome and comfortable, although the fear of becoming obligated keeps all relationships casual, in which no deep feelings need be revealed.

The only person Emily had ever trusted had left her. Her memory of her daddy was an almost hallowed perfection, while her mother had been a terrible disappointment to her. She had not grown up in a circle of unconditional love, but in the confusion that surrounded her father's death. During latency period, between six and ten years, most children normally develop same-sex friendships which enhance their ability to trust others and feel better about themselves. Because of Emily's unusual life experiences, she had been unable to do that.

She was indeed lucky that she had learned to dance and was able to participate in school programs. That may have been her salvation. The activities that adolescents take on become their identity, and, if they become a dancer or a swimmer or a football player, they are much less likely to become a gang member or a "druggie."

The need to recreate the dysfunctional relationships that people have with their parents emerged, and Emily certainly recreated what she had experienced with her mother in the very punitive relationship she had with her first husband. She had chosen, not consciously, a relationship which is the most painful, I believe, that one can experience with her husband, the womanizer. In her second marriage she had instinctively chosen a man who was a father image. Older, stable, and financially secure, he was also more emotionally mature, but he still provided a punishing relationship due to his requiring from her something she was unable to give. In the end he duplicated the experience she'd had with her dad; he left her.

Emily's idea of "making life pleasant for Momma" was more like appeasing and catering to a spoiled child. Emily drove an old car and did without things herself in order to be able to give money to her mother, to take her on trips, and to generally indulge her, which her mother was more than willing to allow. Whenever her mother called, Emily nearly tripped over herself getting to the telephone to see what Momma wanted or needed. Emily had a sad but tender feeling for her mother which was a combination of pity, love, and undefined guilt. Such a combination is typical of one who in childhood could not get the needed affection, attention, and approval.

Emily's work in the therapeutic environment allowed her to learn how to trust another person and also to trust herself. We had to rebuild her very trampled self-esteem, a job that took many months.

Beth Ann's Story

"What I remember most, I guess, is fear. My mother, and my grandmother too, seemed to love to scare me. The incident that first comes to my mind is one day when they took me to the mall, and I was so excited about going that I was jumping all over the place. I couldn't have been more than about three or four years old because I know I wasn't in school yet.

"Instead of making sure that I stayed with them as most mothers would do, they somehow let me wander off and then, to teach me a lesson, they hid from me. I'll never forget how terrified I was when I started looking for them and they were nowhere in sight. I still remember the panic I felt not knowing what to do. I started to cry and it seemed like a long time that I stood there all by myself, although it probably seemed a lot longer than it really was.

"Finally, some lady stopped and she was so sweet to me that it made me cry all the harder; and I couldn't seem to talk, I just cried. It wasn't until two or three more ladies stopped to try and help that my mother and grandmother came out from where they had been standing and watching me become terrified.

"My mother said, 'Now do you think you can stay with us?' I still remember the look on that nice lady's face, and I didn't understand then what it meant; but as I think about it now I realize that she must have been disgusted with the whole scene.

"God, I hung onto my mother's skirt for dear life! She didn't like for me to hold her hand. I guess she really did teach me a lesson, but I had nightmares about that for a long, long time.

"Oh yes, there was this other thing. I'm embarrassed to talk about it, and maybe there was something physically wrong with me; but I always had to go to the bathroom, and my mother never could understand that. She'd always tell me that I had to wait. I think I spent my life waiting until I got somewhere, and I'd just hurt so bad.

"One time I had to go so bad and I just could not stand it any longer. I was in the back seat of the car and I remember thinking that if I just went in the seat, the seats were vinyl, that it would just run back behind it and Mother would never know. I was wrong, it ran right onto the floor in a big puddle and I thought my mother was going to have a stroke—it's a wonder I didn't have a stroke! And then, when we got home she made me go to the barn—we lived in the country—and get in a little tub out there to clean me up. I was just humiliated to death that she wouldn't let me go into the house. And, of course, my brothers just teased me unmercifully about it. I didn't think they were ever going to forget about me doing that awful thing in the back seat.

"I never felt like my mother loved me. I hate to talk about her because she's dead now, and I'm ashamed to tell you that at her funeral I couldn't make myself cry. I tried to, because I thought I was supposed to, but I just couldn't do it. And, even now, I don't feel sorry that she's gone even though I know she couldn't help the way she was because she was sick.

"She was in a mental hospital when she died eight years ago; I was seventeen years old then. But, as a little kid, I didn't know all that, and it probably wouldn't have mattered much to me at that time anyway. All I knew was that she acted as if she was a little kid herself. She would stick her tongue out at me and make faces at me like she just hated me, and it would hurt so bad that I wanted to die. She was so quick to anger and to call me stupid and ugly. She criticized everything I did, everything I said, and I never once remember her saying that she loved me or hugging me or calling me anything sweet. But, you know, I hardly ever cried. All the time, years and years of trying not to cry because she would make fun of me if I did, so I just held it in. I just hate to talk about it or even to think about it because it's just like I'm back there and it is happening all over again. It all happened so long ago, it's hard to believe there could still be so much pain. But I am feeling the hurt right now, just as if it had happened today. Now I cry about it, don't I? I guess I'm really making up for all those years I couldn't cry. I'll bet I'm using up my lifetime share of tears now that I have gotten started.

"As I got older I had so much work to do. I was expected to cook all the meals and do most of the housework, plus go to school. If something had to slide, it would have to be my schoolwork. Mother never knew anything about my school or my grades, and she said that my first duty was my responsibilities at home. I practically raised my little brother because mother was gone so much. I still don't know where she was all the time—she didn't work—but I was still pretty much in charge of the house. But everything I did was wrong and I was always grounded because of it. I remember vacuuming the floors, and I would go over and over them so that she would be pleased, and damned if she couldn't find something that was not perfect every time. She really delighted in punishing me, and I'm serious about that. I hardly ever had a chance to plan anything; but the few times I did, I'd get grounded at the last minute. And it was that pleased look on her face when she did that, I think, that made me feel so bad.

"But I did have my Dad, back when I was little at least. He couldn't stop her from being mean to me or make her love me, but at least he was nice to me. I used to run out to the car to meet him when he would come home, and he'd say, 'What's the matter, honey, did you have a bad day?' And he would pick me up and hold me, and I'd feel better for a while. But I guess that was too good to continue too, because as I got a little older he began to touch me in different ways. At the time I didn't understand why it felt wrong, but of course now I realize it was sexual touching. And he began barging into the bathroom while I was in the tub, saying that he had to make sure I was getting myself clean. Oh, I just hated that! After that all started happening I was afraid of him too, and I began to avoid him. But more than once I woke up in the night and he would be sitting on my bed. Once he tried to touch me down on my panties, but I pulled away from him and I did cry then, I remember, and I said, 'Daddy, please don't do that,' and he stopped. He never bothered me again, but I never forgot that. And always, after that, I slept in clothes, never pajamas or a nightgown. Somehow I had the idea that 'daytime' clothes would protect me, and do you know that, even now, when I go home to visit, as long as I am sleeping in that house, I still sleep in 'daytime' clothes.

"One thing I can say, though, is that I hardly ever got hit and certainly was never beaten. The worse thing my mother ever did was slap me in the face, and that was humiliating, but it really didn't happen very often. So it's not like I was an abused child or anything like that."

Presenting Problem:

Beth Ann had been experiencing extreme anxiety and suffering from panic attacks that were so disabling she had required hospitalization for a short time. Prescribed medication helped her get in control well enough to begin functioning once again. However, that was only the preliminary step that enabled her to begin to get to the bottom of what was triggering her emotional turmoil.

When I began seeing Beth Ann, although the medication had helped her considerably, she was still having the panic attacks, anxiety, depression, rapid pounding heartbeat, hyperventilation, and a terrifying fear that she was dying or going crazy. These are all symptoms of a condition called Agoraphobia. Once this was explained to Beth and a label put on the disorder, she felt tremendous relief. The very fact that her bizarre symptoms had a name seemed to give her hope that she could be helped. This illness is very often misdiagnosed because of its bizarre symptoms and because they are so difficult to explain. Agoraphobia literally means "the fear of open spaces" and can be more accurately described as "the fear of fear." I once heard an analogy which helped me understand more about this strange phobia. If a nonphobic person were being chased by a bear, he would be terrified. The adrenaline would flow and he would probably feel panic. The Agoraphobic feels that same fear but without the bear. Try to imagine what it must be like to experience that kind of terror for absolutely no objective reason. This is what was happening to Beth Ann much of the time.

The first time Beth Ann experienced a panic attack it came "out of the blue." She had been under considerable stress and felt helpless in her ability to resolve the problems in her life, involving job, finances, and her relationships. She had, at one time, had a bout with drug abuse and had managed, with great difficulty, to conquer that problem. However, she was fearful that, with the problems in her life, her sobriety was threatened.

Continual stress in combination with the holding-in of feelings can cause tension to build in the body, finally manifesting in some form of psychosomatic disturbance which may appear as ulcers, high blood pressure, migraine headaches, or other body aches. In the case of the Agoraphobic, the stress overload causes adrenaline to surge through the body and results in a panic attack. Of course, Beth Ann had learned well the fine art of holding in feelings, and, with the fearful consciousness she had developed, her symptoms were quite understandable.

Typically, the background of the Agoraphobic includes a parent who was phobic and one who was authoritarian or overprotective. Beth Ann knows that her mother was mentally disturbed, but she does not know the diagnosis. Quite possibly her mother's illness included phobic disorders, and there is no question that her mother was authoritative.

Her father also contributed to Beth Ann's fearfulness and anxiety. Even though she did not understand, and was confused by, her father's sexual advances, some primal knowledge alerted her that he was being inappropriate. She was extremely fortunate that he did not persist and that she was able to put a stop to his actions. As we know, this is not always the case. But it takes very little sexual inappropriateness to knock Daddy off his parental pedestal. When a child has lost trust in her father, it is a great loss with future repercussions.

Agoraphobics are generally seen by others as outgoing, personable, and having a good sense of humor. They are also above average in intelligence and are creative and imaginative. In fact, it is their active minds and their vivid imaginations which often cause problems with this phobia. They are loyal friends with empathy for others, which are qualities that we regard as positive. An agoraphobic person, however, has a tendency to take the problems of others and make them his or her own. They are warm and sensitive and tend to operate out of their feelings. They are also perfectionistic and, of course, overly critical of themselves. This character sketch, taken from the literature on Agoraphobia, perfectly describes Beth Ann.

She is one of the most beautiful, delicate, and feminine-looking young women you could imagine. You could easily see her in a magazine advertising beauty products. In fact, people who know her have a hard time believing that her insecurity is genuine. It is genuine.

With this disorder as a starting point, Beth Ann and I had our therapeutic work cut out for us; the lion's share of the work was hers to do. Strong phobias or anxiety reactions generally take a long time to heal. The healing comes, in all therapy, from expressing resentments, fears, and archaic anger. However, the phobic patient must also learn to live with, and deal with, their crippling fears and anxieties on a daily basis. Not an easy job.

We were well into our work, and Beth Ann had made considerable progress, when a young man came into her life. She was very attracted to him—and he was definitely pursuing her—but she seemed to be sabotaging the relationship. As we talked it out, she related that he was not like anyone she'd ever been involved with and she felt that she was clearly out of her element.

She was terrified to let herself care too much, for she was sure that as soon as he knew about her past and current problems he would leave her. And she didn't feel able to endure any further battering of her emotions. But the heart is an unruly little animal, and she did become involved with him. Her anxiety and fears reached monumental proportions. The love songs that describe the "pain of love" are all understatements compared to the pain of Beth Ann's love. In her past relationships she had always picked abusive, emotional cripples, with her doing most of the giving and always investing much more, emotionally and financially, than she received. This man was emotionally healthy, attentive, caring, from a traditional family, and financially solvent. Beth Ann didn't even have to pay for their dates—imagine! It's not surprising that she was fearful. She simply had no experience with this kind of relationship and this kind of partner.

We have some innate impulse to recreate the same emotionally dysfunctional relationships in our adult lives that we grew up with, and that is exactly what Beth Ann had been doing for years. Hopefully, she had now sufficiently suffered the negative situations and would be able to enter a mature relationship. It was a very positive step for her to even be attracted to this emotionally healthy man. It was a first for her.

Eventually, the young man began to accompany her occasionally to her sessions, and in that safe setting she was able to share with him the reasons for her insecurity. To her great surprise, he did not drop her and run away. Slowly, very slowly, she began to build a trust in him, in herself, and in their partnership.

Esther's Story

"I felt an indescribable depth of emptiness, loneliness, and fatigue. The emptiness and loneliness are easy to understand, and the fatigue probably came from all the activity I engaged in trying to block out the sounds of my parents when they were fighting. This was literally all of the time that my father was home.

"As a small child I remember riding my tricycle around and around in the living room in circles, and singing some little song over and over, the notes growing louder and louder as if to drown out the ugly noise of my mother's angry voice. I remember her yelling at my father, 'Why can't you ever do anything for me, and why are you always too busy for me?' I also remember her saying, 'You hate me and you hate my child.' I always thought it was funny that she called me 'her child' and never 'our child.' I remember wondering if he was really my father. But worse than the yelling was the thudding and bumping sound that I was sure was my mother being bounced off the walls and, of course, her screaming and crying above it all. I would ride so hard and sing so loud that eventually, exhausted, I would just go to sleep.

"Later, I would wake up to her sobbing, and she was always drinking something; and the more she drank, the more depressed she became. She would vent her anger at my father. Mostly it was because he was away from home so much and because his business was nightclubs; he owned several. She used to confide in me that he had a 'floozy,' and it was the longest time before I knew what a 'floozy' was. She told me that he made tons of money, but that he wouldn't give her a cent, and how she had to scrape and save to keep the household running. And she'd 'be Goddamned if she was going to get a job' when it was his responsibility to provide for his family.

"I rarely saw my father in those days, but, when I did, I remember he wasn't mean to me. It's just that I didn't know him very well. I remember my eighth birthday and how surprised I was when he showed up at the little party my mother had planned. I ran to him and tried to hug him, but he said, 'Esther, you're too old for that sort of behavior now.' I will never forget how embarrassed I was and how bad I felt. After that I never received any physical affection from him. My mother had never been affectionate with me unless I initiated it, and I never again initiated it.

"My parents finally separated when I was nine years old, and, of course, I stayed with my mother. I can't tell you how sick I got of hearing about my father and his 'floozy' and about how he never did anything for her and wouldn't give her any money. I used to think constantly about running away. As I look back now, I realize that she always had money for liquor and cigarettes and, God, she got fat so there must have been enough for food. I guess she was your stereotypical 'Jewish mother,' constantly whining and making herself the martyr. I know she was miserable, and somehow I felt responsible. Why do you suppose I felt responsible?

"During the next few years I became sexually active. I would go to bed with any boy who paid attention to me. I'd had two abortions by the time I was fifteen. I'm sure this all had something to do with the lack of affection I received in my family.

"I rarely saw my father and then only when my mother was present. But then, when I was fifteen, my mother got sick and had to go to the hospital for a long period of time. I was pretty sure it had to do with her alcohol consumption, but that was never quite clear to me. Now I know that she was actually in and out of treatment centers and mental hospitals for the next two years.

"Around that time my father divorced my mother and got temporary custody of me. I went to live with him then, and if you don't think that was a crazy feeling! All those years of hearing what an asshole he was and believing every word my mother had told me. It was a real surprise to find out that he was a nice, gentle man. Unaffectionate, but, still, he was nothing like I had been led to believe. I found out that he had been sending money specifically for me for years and had written me letters that I never got. I also learned that during those fights, when I was little, before he left us, when I thought my mother was getting knocked around, it was really the other way around. She would literally back him into a corner while she was screaming at him and, since he wouldn't touch her, he had been the one getting bounced off the walls. Knowing my mother as I do, I wonder why I didn't figure all this out for myself.

"Shortly after I moved in with my father, he married his 'floozy,' whose real name was Margaret. At first I was appalled, but after I got to know her—I hate to say this—but I could understand why he had left my mother for her. She really is a lovely person and has never been anything but kind to me. If my mother heard me say that she would disown me for sure.

"Anyway, Maggie, as my father calls her, had two children of her own who were eight and eleven years old and, if I had allowed it, we could probably have been a pretty happy family. But, you see, those kids had been around my father most of their lives and thought of him as their own father. They even called him Daddy, something I could never do. I was really an outsider.

"I was so jealous that I behaved just like a spoiled brat. I don't see how any of them could stand me. But, after about the first year, I began to feel a little less uncomfortable in the family and a little happier personally. By the time my mother finally got out of the hospital, I was seventeen and old enough to choose where I wanted to live. I chose to stay with my father and his family. I was getting ready to go away to college by then, which was the excuse I gave my mother. I never could have gone back to live with her. But I'll bet you can imagine the guilt trip she put on me, and, of course, I allowed her to do it.

"When I did go away to school it was the biggest relief of my life, even though she used to call me on the telephone almost every night to complain, and it was just like the old days. She didn't have enough money to live on, which was not true because my father still paid all of her expenses, and she had monthly payments of alimony, I know for a fact. Still, she would call and say, 'You, he gives anything, can't you send me some money? Haven't I always been good to you? Don't you remember how I used to cook for you?'

"I'd say, 'Mother, I don't have any money.' I really didn't have much cash or I probably would have given it to her. And then, if you can believe it, she would say, 'Well, maybe you could borrow some from your friends, I know all those kids you go to school with have plenty of money.' I can't tell you how guilty I felt.

"One summer, my father and Maggie and the kids had planned a trip to Europe and they invited me to go along. I was so excited and looking forward to it very much, but when I told Mother she had a fit because she wanted me to spend the summer with her in New York. That was the first time I ever really stood up to her and said, 'No.' I suggested that she invite her sister so she wouldn't be so lonely, and I will never forget what she said. 'Sure, shove me off on Rose, just as long as you don't have to bother with me. Just so you and your father and that floozy can run off to Europe and to hell with me sweating it out in this city. Summers are so long, Esther.'"

Presenting Problem:

Esther entered therapy at age thirty-five, soon after her fourth divorce, in a state of major depression. All but one of her former husbands were alcoholics, and she had been involved in several other relationships with men who were either alcoholics or compulsive gamblers. She says:

> You wouldn't believe the "scuzzy" guys I have picked, and they have all treated me like hell. It seems like the lousier they are to me, the harder I hang on. I'd probably hang on forever, even though I know how destructive the relationship is, but in the end they always leave me. And then I am left with horrible feelings of desolation and this choking sadness in my throat. But this time I'm feeling something even more terrible and desperate. I feel panic because I know I'm in danger of a breakdown.

Actually, Esther herself was a fairly successful woman. She had finished college and was a computer whiz, which is a miracle considering the pressure and stress with which she was bombarded all through her school years.

She made a lot of money but had spent most of it on the emotional cripples to whom she'd been attracted and who were attracted to her. She was very fortunate to have two well-adjusted, teen-aged sons; also a miracle, given the caliber of the stepfathers to whom they had been subjected.

The boys' father, Sol, was Esther's first and only emotionally healthy husband and had remained very involved in their lives. All of the time Esther spent with her new relationships and marriages allowed him the opportunity to do that. He was intelligent and an athletic kind of man and had encouraged the boys along those lines. Consequently, their extracurricular activities and their scholastic abilities had promoted high self-esteem. They had been able to overcome the effects of the less than desirable adults in their lives.

At the time she entered therapy, Esther was having suicidal thoughts and fears of going crazy. Although the relationships in her life were enough to make anyone "crazy," she apparently did not have the kind of body chemistry that can turn individuals into "psychotics." I referred her to an M.D. who prescribed an anti-depressant medication. During the next two weeks, as the medication stabilized in her system, I saw her several times, each time persuading her to commit to NOT hurting herself until the next time I saw her. We spent hours talking about the dysfunctional upbringing, and she began to see her mother for the manipulative, demanding shrew that she was, whose histrionics had hooked Esther into the guilty feelings that she had carried all of her life. She began to recognize the connection between her helpless mother and the kind of helpless men she had chosen in her life.

She recognized the connection between her physically and emotionally unavailable father and her insatiable need for love. As a teenager, when she was unable to get physical and emotional affection from her parents, she had turned to the only others who offered it. She went to bed with boys in an attempt to feel closeness and in order to be loved. It is very easy for young girls to confuse sex with love.

As a child, Esther had alternated between a dream of life with her parents, reshaped as she would have liked it, and bouts of hopelessness born of the knowledge that the dream was an impossibility. She felt responsible for her Mother's unhappiness because children, in their simplistic thinking, see themselves as the center of the universe, so that, when things are not as they should be, they must make them right. When they are unable to do so, they feel that they are responsible.

After Esther was feeling less depressed with the help of the medication, we began to examine her relationships with men. When she described Sol, it was always with respect and high regard. I began to delve into the reasons that she had divorced him. There was a gentleness about him, she said, that absolutely irritated her to death. It seems he had a very relaxed, easy manner, and it was foreign to her. She was bored with him. There was no tension in the relationship, and she thrived on tension; she'd been raised on it. Anything less was very unexciting. He was also very kind to her, and she had not grown up seeing men and women with an attitude of kindness.

On an intellectual level, Esther knew that she was attracted to unhealthy men but did not know how to make herself feel differently. There was an addictive quality to her relationships, and she was able to recognize this very quickly.

This dependent, obsessive-compulsive kind of "love" is quite similar to addiction to alcohol or other drugs. It is characterized by the panic one feels at the possible absence of the substance (person). A person who has just ended an addictive relationship may suffer withdrawal symptoms and agony greater than a drug addict going cold turkey. There is often physical pain, sleep disturbance, depression, suicidal ideation, and a craving that can be so intense that it drives the individual right back to the source of the addiction. Another trademark of the addictive relationship is that when it is finally over, there is a tremendous feeling of relief and sense of accomplishment.

Because of Esther's emotionally impoverished life as a child, it is easy to understand how this addiction might have developed. *And the first step in controlling any addictive behavior is to recognize it for what it is.* Esther was more than ready to do that and was grateful to be able to understand the basis of her addiction.

Esther's life had been based on emotion, and she had always lived for relationships, passion, excitement, and tension. She had been dependent on people whose love was erratic and who had continually let her down. My suggestion was for Esther to take a rest from relationships for a while. It was time for her to develop a whole self without symbiosis and without the complications fostered by relationships. Independence is a necessity in emotionally healthy relationships, and Esther had never learned what independence was all about. But she was a willing student and set about this task with an excitement that was typical of her.

Celia's Story

"I always said I should write a book about my childhood but I didn't think I'd ever really get a chance to do that. I thought about it a lot though and I would have called it 'Loving Hatred.' When you asked me about the feelings I remember, that's what comes to mind.

"My mother did not love me, of that I am sure. I don't know why she didn't. I used to ask her all the time but she just ignored the question. I always hoped she'd say that I was silly and of course she loved me, but that never happened. She constantly compared me to my older sister and, no matter how well I did, it was not good enough. Once, I brought home two D's on my report card and I got a terrible whipping for that. I may have needed it, she said I did, but, oh Lord how she used to beat me with that leather strap; and I was so stubborn that I refused to cry, and that just made her madder, so she'd just scream and go crazy. Anyway, when I got my next report card, I was so happy I could hardly wait to get home to show her that I'd brought both D's up to B's. I can never forget what she said. 'Well, it's a damn good thing but it's no more than what I expect of you. You do realize that your sister made straight A's, don't you?' I tried so hard to please her but it was not possible. It's still not possible, but I keep on trying. I'd give anything in the world for her to love me.

"My mother always called me a liar. No matter what I said, it was a lie. Sometimes I'd lie just to see if that's what I had to do for her to believe me. That didn't work either. And she used to say that I had a big chip on my shoulder. I remember standing in front of the mirror wondering what a chip was and where it was and why I couldn't see it.

"I had a stepfather, Bert, who was the only Daddy I ever knew. My mother used to go out drinking nearly every night, and they fought about that quite a bit. Bert usually stayed home with my sister and me. He used to make me do sexual things with him, but I never told Mother because I knew she'd say I was lying. Besides, it was the only special attention I got, and I guess it felt like love to me. This is where the 'loving hatred' comes in. I felt like what we did was wrong, and I felt guilty; but I think I loved him and hated me.

"My mom usually came home 'falling down' drunk and crying that nobody loved her. One night I remember getting down on my knees and hugging her and crying that I loved her. She just pushed me down and said; 'Not you stupid.' Shortly after that, she and Bert got a divorce, and I had mixed feelings about that because he'd been an important part of my crazy life. I always knew he'd be there, and that was, somehow, comforting to me. I thought things might get better after he was gone but they got worse. Mom was hardly ever home; and when she was, she was either drunk and crying or bitching at me. She began saying that it was my fault that she'd had to get the divorce. I don't know why she said that, I never told about the ugly things that Bert and I had done. I'd tried my best to forget about all that stuff. It seemed to me that she knew, though, and I felt so guilty.

"At fourteen, I married my twenty-one-year-old boyfriend and thought that finally someone would love me. But he was almost a carbon copy of my mother. He was never satisfied with anything I did or said or how I looked or what I did in bed. And, God, how I hated having sex with him. Of course, I got pregnant right away; and then he left, and I never saw him again. I took my newly born son and went back to live with my mother because there was nothing else for me to do. Life with her was worse than ever, because then I had that poor little baby to raise; and she found fault with everything I did with him. I was such a child myself that I took out all of my frustration on him. As I look back on that time, I wonder how that little boy lived through the treatment he got from me. I treated him just like my mother had treated me, maybe worse. I had thought that by leaving home and getting married, I'd be free; now I was more trapped than ever.

"I began doing a lot of heavy drugs and selling them, thinking that I would get rich and be able to take care of myself. But the more money I made, the more drugs I bought for myself, and it was a vicious circle. This went on for years. I'd move in and out of my mothers house, always leaving my son behind. She eventually got custody and now, fifteen years later, I only see him once or twice a year. Meanwhile, I married another lousy guy and had two more kids. Now we're divorced, and I don't have much choice but to place the girls in foster care until I can get myself together.

Presenting Problem:

I began seeing Celia shortly after she was released from the hospital following a serious suicide attempt. She later confided that it had been her fourth try and that she'd had every intention of dying each time. When, after several sessions, she told me about the sexual abuse, she broke down and cried and said that it was the first time she'd ever been able to share this. She seemed surprised at how angry she was with Bert and with her mother. She said that she'd seen Bert over the years and had often wanted to say something to him about the incest but felt too scared. When asked what was so scary, she said, "I guess I was afraid he'd deny it all and then I'd wonder if I was crazy." For several weeks we explored the idea of confronting Bert and, while I was careful not to push her, Celia clearly could not get the thought out of her mind. She finally came to one of her sessions, sat down, and calmly said, "Well, I did it." She looked like a new person, and I knew exactly what she had done. She had gone to his place of business and said, "You and me are gonna talk." He gave no resistance, she said—he'd probably been expecting this for some time. She told him that he had just about ruined her life and she'd like to kill him for what he had done to her. Bert was quiet for some time, and then said, "You know how things were between me and your Mama, Celia, what could I do?" She answered, "You could have kept your goddamned pants on." Bert immediately said, "I know it, and I want you to know that I'm sorry about everything I did."

Celia could not explain the tremendous relief she experienced, and I can't explain it either. The typical attitude of people when asked to confront a parent about atrocities such as incest is that, no matter what the abusive parent says, nothing will change what happened. My only answer is that if someone spills grape juice on your new white carpet, probably nothing will remove the stain. However, somehow, if the person is genuinely sorry and tells you so, your anger will not develop into unresolvable resentment. In time you may even be able to forgive that person, and you won't be left with a crippling rage that spills over onto every facet of your life. To date, Celia has been unable to talk with her mother about her childhood. She is working toward that, but the thought of making her mother angry is overwhelming. Just as in childhood, she continues to look to "the guilty party"—the abusing parent—for comfort and support, a trait common to most emotionally and physically abused children.

Carrie's Story

"I remember feeling lonely, and I remember a *lot* of fear. Both my parents were ministers in a very rigid fundamentalist church and were so busy out 'ministering' to their flock that we five kids got left alone to root for ourselves. I was the youngest—ten years younger than my closest sister. She and two other sisters had to take care of me, and believe me they did *not* try to hide the resentment they felt about that. Sometimes they could be pretty mean. My brother, who was fifteen when I was born, loved to carry me around hanging by my feet just to listen to me squeal. I'd be so embarrassed because everyone could see my panties.

"It's not that they really abused me, but they just didn't like me very much. I knew it and felt miserable all the time. I used to cry for my mother constantly—it's no wonder the girls hated me so much.

"My parents always went away every summer for seminars and training sessions, and I had to stay with my grandparents on the farm, without even the company of my sisters, and they were even busier than my parents, if that's possible, and that was the loneliest time of all. God, I hated summertime.

"When my parents did take me along with them anywhere, it was always to the church, and, from the earliest time, I remember I had to sit quietly and listen to the sermon. I had no idea what was being said except that it was being said very loudly. I did understand what it meant to "burn" though, and the fear of "burning in Hell forever" kept me terrified day and night. If I dared fall asleep in the service, my dad would tell me that God was mad at me and if he got mad enough I would burn in Hell forever. If I didn't say my prayers right, I would burn in Hell forever. If I didn't pick up my shoes, I would burn in Hell forever. I was so scared that at night I couldn't go to sleep, sometimes for hours. When I did sleep I'd wake up with such awful nightmares I'd just lie there and shiver.

"Because I was the youngest, I had a lot to live up to and never could seem to be quite as good as *someone*. My parents were extremely critical, and I not only had to live up to their expectations but those of everyone in the whole damn church. This went on for eighteen years until I finally went away to college. I'd always been an honor student—God, I was so scared I'd go to Hell if I didn't make all A's that I was obsessed with being perfect.

"But when I got to college I was obsessed with everything *but* making A's. I discovered alcohol and marijuana; I discovered dancing and partying; I discovered sex and became involved in one obsessive, addictive kind of relationship right after another. *And* I became an obsessive atheist.

"I did stay in school—somehow—I swear I don't know how. But I got my degree. At least I did something right, although my parents were not able to find time to come to my graduation. I can't tell you how much that hurt. Here I was, a kid from a family of seven people and I had not one guest at my graduation. They were very displeased with me, they said, because I was not the honor student they knew I could be. But, of course, they had never been pleased with me in twenty-two years—even when I *was* an honor student—and after all, I did graduate. Wouldn't you think they could have at least sent me a Goddamn card?"

Presenting Problem:

When twenty-four year old Carrie came for therapy, she had just about every obsessive-compulsive behavior you can think of. She had an eating disorder; she abused alcohol and other drugs; she was a workaholic-perfectionist; she smoked cigarettes one after another; she'd had terribly destructive relationships, one after another; and she had recently made a suicide attempt that very nearly killed her. When she got out of the hospital, she decided that she wanted to live after all and, as is the case with many obsessive-compulsive people, entered therapy with a vengeance to by-God get well: Right *now*!

People who have obsessive-compulsive behaviors were almost always raised by rigid, controlling parents and grow into adults who feel they must rigidly control *themselves* and their own environment. Eating habits, drug habits, work habits are all controllable by an individual.

There are always some old, unresolved angers, and the underlying emotion of anger, as stated earlier, is generally fear and guilt. And heaven knows, Carrie had been raised with an abundance of fear and guilt.

Until I began seeing Carrie I had never considered the notion of abuse around religious fear. However, after hearing her heartbreaking story and seeing the devastating results of this walking obsessive-compulsive survivor, I began to question my clients a little more closely about their spiritual backgrounds. I have heard incredible accounts of fearful experiences at the hands of parents, relatives, Sunday School teachers, parochial school teachers, nuns, and ministers.

I also recalled an incident in my own childhood in which a Sunday School teacher told my class of five year olds, "When you die you turn to dust." That may seem like a very minor statement, but it was enough to scare me half to death. I remember crying every night for what seemed like forever to me. I don't think I ever told my mother what was wrong with me. That was only a one-time incident. It's hard to imagine the magnitude of Carrie's fears.

She started her work in therapy, as you might imagine, with very structured goals about her drinking, her bulimia, the stress she was causing for herself. However, it had not occurred to her that she might need to experience some feelings about her parents—their absence and rigidity, the fear they had provoked, and their constant criticism. She thought she *had* expressed anger when she became so rebellious in college, and, indeed, that was a form of anger. But it had been directed at the wrong person—at herself, with very self-destructive behavior, and she was suffering the consequences.

For many hours, Carrie sat with me and talked about the mistreatment and neglect as though she was discussing a birthday party, incongruously laughing and shrugging her shoulders and saying, "Isn't this incredible?" What was incredible was that she never displayed an ounce of anger. She did express sadness and guilt and fear, and those are all emotions that do need to be expressed; but they are negative emotions that drag one down. Anger is a healing emotion, and when we get to that point we begin to feel better and more positive about ourselves. When we can feel indignant about bad treatment, we somehow seem to feel more worthwhile.

That is what Carrie finally did. She got good and mad. She practiced for weeks what she wanted to say to her parents. She wrote them letters, which she edited many times until she got them just right, and then she put them away. It was not necessary to mail them. The therapy was in the writing. In many cases confrontation is very constructive and healing but in others it may prove too threatening. At that point, direct confrontation was too threatening for Carrie.

VII

Steps to Recovery

There are many steps to recovery and many paths to get you there, but *you* must take the first step. The following are widely acknowledged as the most effective steps in recovering from a serious emotional injury of any kind.

1. Stop the Denial
2. Work Through the Pain, Anger, and Grief
3. Attend Group Therapy
4. Form a Support Group
5. Replace Roles With Relationships
6. Overcome Obsessive-Compulsive Behavior
7. Write it Down!
8. Try to Remember
9. Trust in a Higher Power
10. One Last Thing—Balance!

1. Stop the Denial

Many people move through life in a great deal of psychic pain and are actually unaware that they can feel otherwise. The first and undoubtedly the most important step in any recovery process is to *define the problem*. That sounds simple enough, doesn't it?

Well, it's not exactly simple, because it means that we must stop the denial, and denial is the single largest obstacle in any recovery program. Our denial system serves as a psychological wall of protection. It is one of the defense mechanisms we use in order to protect ourselves from pain and suffering. In alcoholic families, for example, it's often said that the members deny and ignore the problem as they would ignore an elephant sitting in the living room.

We've used our denial system all of our lives and it has served us well—at least we think it has. Therefore, it is with a great deal of reluctance that we give it up. But we *must* give it up. While walls appear to protect us, in actuality they isolate us. Emotional isolation is one of the most debilitating and most common symptoms of adult survivors of child abuse.

No, giving up the denial system is not a simple matter. It builds up over a long period of time and does not break apart easily. It occurs in stages.

Most people begin by educating themselves. You're already doing that by reading self-help books like this one and others that are on the market. Maybe you're tuning into talk shows and other presentations which address emotional growth. There is also an abundance of workshops you can attend.

The next stage should be to take some time to look honestly at your life as a stranger would. Look at your current life and look at the life you shared with your family of origin. Be as objective as possible and examine the circumstances surrounding your current symptoms. This is mandatory to the rest of your recovery program.

One must acknowledge if beatings were too severe or if sexual advances were inappropriate. One must face the fact if deprivation of needed and deserved affection, attention, and approval did exist in his or her childhood. The facts must finally be acknowledged, even in the face of respect and love for hard-working, well-meaning parents, parents whose own life experiences may have resulted in your neglect or deprivation. Some may have to admit that a passive parent failed to protect them from abuse by the other parent. This is sometimes the most difficult behavior of all to label as abuse but is often just as anger-provoking and hurtful as any of the other forms.

Don't rush through this step, thinking that you have to instantly forgive. You're not ready for that yet. When you forgive too quickly, you cut off your external avenues for working through the pain, anger, and grief. I warned you that the process is not simple. You have some other work to do before you can reclaim the power that is yours.

2. Work Through the Pain, Anger, and Grief

The next step is to recognize the need and to reach out for help. Recovery does not occur alone. You may be saying to yourself, "I thought this was a self-help book! Now she says I have to go get therapy."

If this seems like a cop-out to you, it's not meant to be, and I apologize. Please let me explain.

Therapy *is* healing oneself. And, believe me, it is hard work, not for the therapist, but for the individual. It's not much fun digging up old memories that are painful, *and*, if I knew of a way for you to skip over this portion of the recovery process, I would share it with you.

Now you may be saying, "I can't afford a psychiatrist!" Well, that's probably not what you need at all. Affordable psychotherapy is available to almost everyone. Social workers and psychologists work in private practice with people from all socio-economic classes and all racial and ethnic backgrounds. All major cities have mental health clinics, often subsidized by the United Way with a sliding scale of fees. Many times, after a few individual sessions, the therapist will suggest group therapy, which is considerably less expensive and is without question the treatment of choice.

The next thing you may be saying is, "I am not going to any damn group." I know I'm making a lot of projections about what you might be saying to yourself, but, if I'm right, you're not alone. Because of the isolative tendencies of adult survivors of child abuse, the mere mention of group therapy makes them want to run like a jack rabbit. This is the very reason that individual therapy is initially preferable for as long as it takes to build a bond and some measure of trust. But please read on and let me explain the group experience.

3. Attend Group Therapy

Again, recovery does not occur alone. It's very important to have a support system, and it needs to be with others who are in recovery. The therapy group resembles a family in many respects, often led by a male and female co-therapy team in a deliberate effort to simulate the parental figures. The adult survivor of child abuse enters therapy with a history of highly unsatisfactory experiences in his or her first and most important group setting, the family of origin. Members generally interact with leaders and other members of the group much as they once interacted with their parents and siblings. However, this time the behavioral patterns are confronted and challenged, and new ground rules are set. The old, familial conflicts are relived and this time, relived in a healthier fashion. Working through problems with the therapist and co-members is also, in essence, working through the unfinished business of the past.

In my experience, when clients look back over the course of the group therapy experience, they almost always credit the other group members as having been very important in their own improvement process.

Dr. Irvin Yalom, long recognized as one of the leading experts on the subject of group therapy, states that one of the most important factors in group therapy is observing the improvement of other group members. Patients enter therapy, he says, with the disquieting thought that they are unique in their wretchedness and that they alone have unacceptable problems. Like other curative factors of group therapy, their universality cannot be discovered separately. To put it more simply, we need a support system, and it *works best* with others who are recovering and serious about their own emotional growth.

When adult survivors of child abuse engage in group therapy, typically it is the first time they have dared to discuss their experiences with anyone other than perhaps their primary therapist. Virtually all of the participants have the universal reactions of relief and release as they are finally able to disclose the deep, dark secret of their abusive pasts. It's as if the world has been lifted right off their shoulders, and more than one of my clients have expressed their feelings in those very words.

Goals of Group Therapy

The goals that I believe necessary for success in this area of treatment, and those I have adopted for my own group work, are as follows:

a. The group must provide a safe, supportive environment in which members can share experiences and feelings of the past and present.

b. The group must relieve the isolationism that is so common to adult survivors of child abuse.

c. The group must provide the encouragement that will enable its members to explore and express long-suppressed emotions in an appropriate manner.

d. The group must create a consistently predictable environment that allows members to learn trust.

e. The group must enable members to practice decision making and problem solving, which will allow them to gain control of their lives.

f. The group must provide a setting in which members can practice and experiment with new behaviors and interpersonal communication skills, enabling them to develop close personal relationships.

Keep in mind that although each goal is discussed singly, the factors are interdependent and do not occur separately.

Further Explanation of These Goals

a. The group must provide a safe, supportive environment in which members can share the experiences and feelings of the past and present:

This goal is partly directed toward the group leader who must set the stage and create a trusting, safe, therapeutic environment in which each member is encouraged to be an active participant. However, each member must also assume the responsibility of providing trust, safety, support, and courage for one another and must know that whatever is shared will be totally confidential.

This is the setting in which an individual's low self-worth can be addressed. With encouragement from the leader and from the other members, individuals can begin the tedious process of changing their opinions about themselves. Each member is asked, "What qualities are there about yourself that are positive?" "What do you like about yourself?" In the beginning, many can find absolutely nothing to recommend themselves. But, slowly, reluctantly, some strengths are almost always identified, and the list begins to grow. Upon these strengths, a foundation is built and a new self-image can be constructed.

b. The group must relieve the isolationism that is so common to adult survivors of child abuse:

Most children have a need to be like all the rest of the kids. Therefore, when they go to school or to a day care center and discover that their home environment is not like that of all the rest of the kids, the great secretive cycle begins. They may have at some point confided in someone and been accused of lying or simply disbelieved. Or they may have had their disclosures used against them in some way. For example, one client was able to share the terrible feelings she experienced when she told her favorite aunt that her father was insisting that she watch pornographic films with him and his friends. Her aunt, who had been an important part of the client's support system, began to avoid her. Relatives as well as outsiders are often reluctant to become involved in "other people's business."

Such experiences reinforce the need for secrecy. The group experience is often the first exposure clients may have had to others who have had similar or even worse experiences themselves. And when one member breaks the secretive cycle it is as though a dam has tumbled down, and all of the stories pour out one after the other. The release of tension these people feel is often very moving to the whole group and produces a closeness never before experienced. For the discloser, however, having made himself so vulnerable, it is also very threatening and frightening. This is another crucial reason that the safe, supportive environment must be established.

c. The group must provide the encouragement that will enable its members to explore and express long-suppressed emotions in an appropriate manner:

Members are not only given permission to talk about their abusive experiences, but are encouraged to do so. Most of these experiences are quite emotional, and members need to know that it is therapeutic for them to express the hurt or the rage they have kept to themselves for such a long time.

Crying is a task and part of the healing process as well, and so members are generally asked, "Have you been able to cry about this?" "Have you been able to express your anger about this?" But adult survivors of child abuse have the incredible ability to block out their feelings, since it was part of the way they as children learned to survive. But if blocking out pain, anger, and other negative feelings sounds blissful, one must realize that, in order for that to happen, the opposite feelings such as happiness, joy, and closeness to others are also blocked, making for a very dreary existence.

Wilson (1980) has identified this phenomenon as *psychic numbing*. When the person relates and describes a brutal incident with no affect, as though he or she were talking about a trip to the grocery store, the leader and the other members of the group must point this out and confront, asking "How was that for you then?" and, "How does it feel now while you're talking to us about it?" Getting a real response is often quite a chore. However, over time, in a safe environment, feelings can be legitimized, and the members can allow themselves to acknowledge and express their very well-guarded emotions.

d. The group must create a consistently predictable environment that allows members to learn trust:

One of the most typical characteristics of the abusive family is the tremendous inconsistency of parental behavior. A child's actions may be met on any given day with laughter and good humor while the same actions next day may be met with severe punishment. Because of this the child grows up never knowing what to expect, so it is not surprising that as an adult he or she would find it difficult to trust themselves or others.

An important job for the group leader is to establish order and structure in the group and to provide consistent responses. Adult survivors of child abuse have an unconscious tendency to test others, often in the form of baiting, to see how they will react. The leader must react with unconditional positive regard, not necessarily toward the behavior, but with respect and caring for the individual. Emotions are extremely fragile in the beginning phases of recovery.

e. The group must enable members to practice decision making and problem solving, which will allow them to gain control of their lives:

Because of the feelings of helplessness and powerlessness with which abuse victims are plagued, their decision-making and problem-solving skills are generally almost nonexistent or are maladaptive at best. In the group, problems are clearly focused upon, examined, and discussed, allowing members to practice various alternative solutions and behaviors. Too often adult survivors of child abuse have had no opportunity in their development to experience this. Instead, they have simply made impulsive decisions with no consideration given to alternative options.

Another effective tool used in group therapy is role-playing. This gives the members a chance to try out new and unfamiliar behaviors, and dialogues which can provide them with new patterns for dealing with life experiences rather than continuing their old, nonfunctional style.

f. The group must provide a setting in which members can practice and experiment with new behavior and interpersonal communication skills, enabling them to develop close personal relationships:

Remember the old saying, "Children should be seen and not heard," and, "Don't speak until you're spoken to"? These sayings are common parental commands in many families and the messages conveyed are that what a child has to say is not very important or worthwhile.

To most mothers, a good child is a quiet child. In extremely abusive families the messages are much less subtle. Children from these families may think, "If I open my mouth, I might just get my head knocked off." Mothers in Shelters for Battered Women, where the stress and tension is very high, typically tell their children, "Shut your mouth or you're going to bed." Physical punishment is not allowed in most shelters—otherwise, the threats would be much worse than "go to bed." The point is that these children grow up thinking that "to talk is bad; to ask for what I want is bad; to cry when I am needy is more than just bad." Most of these mothers are so frightened and angry that they rarely speak to the children at all unless in harsh, negative tones.

Consequently, adult survivors of child abuse rarely develop good conversational abilities, and their communication skills are limited. These deficits affect all areas of their lives, including jobs, school performance, interpersonal relationships, and certainly their love lives. But communication is a learned behavior and can be learned at any age. Just as you would learn any new skill, the way one learns new social behavior is to practice it. And in practicing this new behavior, developing close personal relationships becomes a new possibility.

In the group setting we can address all of these issues by providing the opportunity to practice communicating and conversing, exchanging and sharing. We start by asking members to describe fearful memories and then ask the group to discuss the ways they would behave in a similar situation. It is always amazing for the discloser to discover that other members, as well as the group leader, have similar reactions and anxieties. It is a valuable insight for a person to discover that he or she is not alone in feeling shy and awkward. This is another important area where role playing serves as a useful technique. It can be used in order to test new ways of conversing in a social setting as well as job interviews and other anticipated life experiences calling for appropriate verbal skills.

The group is the vehicle that provides the opportunity for all these new experiences. The group must create a safe, supportive environment and allow its members to learn to trust, to share, to problem-solve, to communicate, and to build self-worth. In this way, the group becomes the agent of change.

Within these goals for therapy, basically, lie the tools for recovery. They are all interrelated and often overlap each other. However, when the goals are met, each member should have accomplished some crucial steps toward a much happier and healthier life. He or she will have acknowledged that the childhood treatment by primary parental figures was dysfunctional and inappropriate, and that there was no need for them, as children, to have been treated as they were. In other words, they were not to blame for what happened to them.

In making this discovery comes the first "overlap" because it is important to place the responsibility where it really belongs with the parents who were in command of their formative years—and to allow themselves to experience the feelings that accompany this foreign revelation. People often wonder why they need to dredge up all the old hurts. "It won't change what happened," they say. "Besides, it has taken me years to forget about it all. . . . Anyway, the past is past!"

And they are right, the past is past, but it is also prologue, and the painful childhood memories too often flood us against our will. No one with a future is without a past; and the more insecure the past, the more insecure the present. It is the dirty job of the therapist to pull people back into the feelings they thought they had forgotten, in order to work toward a secure future. I am not suggesting that after this acknowledgement the anger must be carried around for the rest of one's life, or that people should never again see or speak to their abusive parents. On the contrary, I am suggesting that the anger must be acknowledged; after a few times of expressing the feelings, the emotion can be put into its proper perspective.

As the victim gains control over a particular emotion, he or she has a sense of peaceful relief and is almost always able to forgive the parent and to go forward with his or her own life. At that point the person ceases to be "the victim" and becomes "the survivor."

For those of you who are unable to forgive and resolve, and there are many, the end result of recovery must be different. If you simply cannot coexist with your parents *and* your mental health; you have no choice but to choose your mental health.

A few years ago I attended a lecture by Dr. Janet Woititz, author of *Adult Children Of Alcoholics*, in which she made this statement: "We all spend our lives recovering from our childhood!" That is really what therapy is all about—recovery from one's childhood. Harold Bloomfield also addresses this in his book, *Making Peace With Your Parents*. I recommend both of these books.

4. Form A Support Group

A person need not be in severe trauma to benefit from a support group. Although I believe it is preferable to have a professional group leader, you may decide to form an informal group without a leader. If you do, that's certainly all right, too. This decision should depend upon the nature and degree of your emotional difficulty. Here are some guidelines you should follow:

a. Six to eight members is a good group size. More than eight is a crowd.

b. Each member should commit to at least eight weekly sessions.

c. A specific stated agreement concerning confidentiality must exist.

d. Understand that the group is not a place to give advice to others, but a safe place in which to share experiences and feelings.

e. Follow the six goals for therapy presented earlier in this chapter.

Maybe you are already in therapy and that is why you're reading this book and others like it. You're educating yourself, getting information. Good for you! You're on your way!

5. Replace Roles With Relationships

One of the most important phases of recovery has to do with the relationships one has with others. Chapter V on Role Playing Modes addresses many of the dysfunctional, often addictive, kinds of relationships common to adult survivors of child abuse. This is generally the issue that has brought the individual into therapy in the first place. Unbelievable as it may seem, people do have the tendency to recreate, over and over again, the same crazy, dysfunctional relationships they have experienced with their crazy, dysfunctional parents. You may be thinking, "No, not me! I would *not* want to do that!" Well, of course you wouldn't, at least not on a conscious level. However, almost all of us do repeat life patterns in some way. The lifestyle is familiar to us, and the familiar is much less frightening and elicits less anxiety than the unfamiliar. In the field of mental health this is referred to as "repetition compulsion." In addition, the adult survivor of child abuse many times unconsciously chooses to repeat a familiar abusive relationship in order to relive the old scene and maybe this time get it right.

Not until we begin to change our beliefs are we able to recognize these patterns and put a stop to them. When we get ourselves into a healthier state of mind, we begin to attract and be attracted to healthier partners. And, since most of us do not want to spend our lives alone, therein lies one of the real sources of happier living.

Robin Norwood discusses this subject in depth in her book *Women Who Love Too Much* and suggests forming one's own group either with or without a therapist as facilitator. She introduced the idea that women who recognize themselves as having the same symptoms described in her book place notices in the newspaper in order to find other women who are interested in forming a group. The result has been phenomenal. *Women Who Love Too Much* groups have sprung up all over the country. I have led a few of these myself, and each time the "women who love too much" come to a realization that an important task for their recovery is *making peace with their parents*—a natural evolution.

6. Overcome Obsessive-Compulsive Behavior

Another common symptom that survivors of child abuse bring to treatment is some kind of obsessive-compulsive behavior. Obsessive-compulsive is a fancy term which simply means that we seem unable to control ourselves in regard to our addictive patterns. We seem compelled to be obsessive. A few of the patterns that are problematic, along with addictive relationships, include work, food, alcohol and other drugs, spending, exercise, sex, chocolate, caffeine, and nicotine. There are others. You may want to add to this list. The interesting part of this is that not one of these activities is particularly dangerous in and of itself. For example, food is one of the essentials of life. We must have it. However, eating food in excess is very harmful and can even contribute to our death. It's one thing to run a mile or two every day, but the obsessive-compulsive person may run ten or twelve miles twice a day. So it is not the addictive agent that is the focus here. Rather, it is the obsessive-compulsive way in which it is used that is harmful to us.

Obsessive-compulsive behavior seems to have something to do with a central issue; that issue is control. Those who grew up in abusive families received distorted messages about themselves. Feelings of powerlessness were often so overwhelming that power and control are now crucial in their adult lives. When other things are out of control, then how one works, eats, smokes, gambles, etc., is something that can be controlled without interference from others. When one or more of these activities becomes obsessive, the individual can have serious problems.

And since the final step of recovery is changing the problem behavior, we need to look at how to do that. For more than fifty years now, there has been an organization that is the primary instrument in the recovery of a multitude of alcohol and other drug addicts. It's name is Alcoholics Anonymous, and the twelve-step program around which it thrives is now the basis for many other programs. The twelve-step groups are, without a doubt, the most successful programs available. They are nonprofit and absolutely free for the taking. The other steps I have outlined are crucial to understanding your past and current self, and people feel tremendously better after having done that. However, without making the important life changes, recovery is only *partially* completed. Many people are fearful about attending a meeting for the first time, and they often shop around before they find the right group. When they get into the recovering community, that becomes easy to do. What they must know is that they will not be required to say a word, other than their first name, until they are perfectly comfortable in doing so. Being there and listening *is* participation, and that is enough for many, sometimes for a long while.

For more information, there is a directory to twelve-step and other support services in chapter 11.

7. Write It Down!

I'm a great believer in writing as a therapeutic tool, and I don't just ask my clients to do it; I give them a choice as to which way they want to do it, because it's that important.

a. Letters: They can write letters to their parents or other abuser, editing and rewriting them until they are perfectly satisfied that everything has been covered: What their parents did or did not do that was so damaging to them, how it affected them as children and how it affected them as adults—and spelling out just exactly what they want from them now.

b. Lists: Some very structured kinds of people prefer to make lists of their resentments, and that's all right too, as long as they are specific about the act and the effect it had on their lives.

c. Stories: Some people actually write their life stories. I teasingly tell them I want them to write my next book for me. In actuality, I probably have enough life stories for three or four next books.

Many people do all three, once they finally get started. When I introduce the idea of writing, they often initially say, "Oh gosh, I don't think I can do that," and then come in the next week with seventeen pages, saying, "I can't believe I did it, but once I got started I just couldn't stop."

I really can't explain the therapeutic magic of writing; maybe it just helps to clarify ideas, crystallize thoughts and feelings. For some, the act of writing is just a dress rehearsal for a face-to-face confrontation. For others, mailing it to their abuser is the only confrontation they can manage. For still others, the therapy is in the act of writing, and they simply put it away.

(See the Appendix for examples of what victims of serious child abuse wrote to their parents as part of their reconciliation with themselves.)

8. Try To Remember

Where childhood abuse has been severe, repression of memories is often the result. When such children become adults they may be totally unaware, or only dimly aware, of the past experience, having stored it in the unconscious. For this reason, many incidents of sexual abuse go unreported and untreated.

But, says Sally Flagg Wallis, noted Dallas hypnotherapist, our unconscious is a "smart cookie" and doesn't allow important information to go unnoticed forever, even if the abuse occurred before we were verbal. The feelings surrounding these incidents, however, are likely to be expressed behaviorally. (See Chapter 10 for a list of behavioral signs that may be indicative of sexual abuse.)

When an abuse victim becomes motivated to gain greater self-understanding and enters into therapy, he or she may consciously want to know what happened and may even develop an overwhelming desire to "find the missing pieces of the puzzle." Hypnotism is one technique that may bridge the gap between unconscious and conscious memory to reach into these forgotten experiences.

Wallis warns, however, that sometimes the unconscious mind says, "No." And then hypnotherapy simply will not be successful. The natural instinct of every human being is self-protection, and so when the unconscious mind resists making some memories public, it is demonstrating its capacity to be self-protective.

But if the answer from the unconscious mind is "Yes," then this is what occurs: The subject enters an altered state of consciousness in which the conscious and unconscious minds overlap. The conscious mind is still the dominant force, but the unconscious rises up to overlap part of it. This overlap is where the conscious mind is distracted or "tuned out," allowing the repressed information to come to the surface.

9. Trust In A Higher Power

There is a final, very important phase of the recovery process. It's something that can turn people off, but I think it needs to be addressed. When people are suffering from the long term effects of a dysfunctional family, it is very easy for their spirituality to deteriorate. Abuse, whether physical or emotional, creates an isolation of the most profound kind—isolation from support systems that help give the courage we need for personal and emotional growth. But when an abused person who has never learned to trust anyone or anything is asked to trust a higher power, it is often very difficult. For so much of their lives, the "Higher Power" to them was the abusive or neglectful parent, so this is understandable.

I believe that in order for recovery to proceed, one must reconnect with, or develop a new relationship with, the spiritual self. Many people have said to me, "I don't want any part of that—I've had it up to here with churches and I've heard enough Hellfire and Damnation to last a lifetime."

I understand and respect their feelings. But spirituality does not necessarily mean traditional religion. It means spirituality in whatever sense that is meaningful to the person as an individual. For some it may be through meditation, finding a teacher, or simply getting in touch with nature. For others, it may mean searching out a church or study group with which they can relate. Whatever gives you peace, whatever gives you serenity, is worth its weight in gold.

10. One Last Thing—Balance!

Adult survivors of child abuse often have such deep feelings and react so intensely that trivialities are exaggerated completely out of proportion. In order to compensate, they may have learned to detach themselves so as not to feel or care at all, but this does not have to be an all-or-nothing reaction. The trick is not to feel and care so much that it makes you crazy, nor so little that you are unable to enjoy interpersonal relationships and life in general.

Another trick is to learn to disregard the irrelevant and focus on positive goals. Don't sweat the small stuff!

Then set your priorities. Above all, don't be too hard on yourself! Instead of trying to become perfect now, why not start by setting a nonabusive goal for yourself; have a fairly balanced life *most* of the time.

Since you've already heard the essential message of this book, you've probably identified with some part of it; and I'm sure that the realization has caused you some degree of pain. I sincerely hope that you have a better understanding of yourself than you did when you began reading. I congratulate you on making this step in your emotional growth and urge you to continue by following the recommended steps for recovery.

Good Luck!

VIII

Follow Up

I continue to follow up on the progress of my clients even after they terminate therapy. I like to know that they are still functioning well. They even seem to feel the need to give me an update periodically. I wish every ending were happy; however, I cannot honestly report that to be true. Some clients are unable or unwilling to withstand the pain of growth. This is understandable and is one of the crippling effects of childhood abuse.

Carrie

Carrie terminated her therapy several months ago. She had her eating disorder under control reasonably well and was continuing in AA and OA.

I ran into her a few weeks ago, and she introduced me to her fiancé, who seemed like a very nice person. Carrie told me that she's happier than she's ever been in her life. Guess where she's getting married—in church!

Celia

After Celia confronted her stepdad, she felt that her therapy was complete and stopped seeing me for several months. When she returned, she was able to focus on the relationship with her mother and did subsequently confront her as well. She reported that it was a very emotional time for both of them when Celia told her that she'd never felt loved. Her mom put her head down on her arms and cried and sobbed for a long time. Then she told her that she was sorry—that she'd never been able to bond with her because Celia was such a difficult baby. It seems that she'd cried and screamed for hours at a time and had not allowed cuddling. According to her mother, Celia was very hyperactive as a toddler, and her defiance had nearly driven her mother crazy with frustration. She said that she *did* love her as a child but had remained furious with her for years.

Celia told her mother about Bert and the sexual abuse, and again she cried. She told Celia that her sister had come to her with a similar story and that she hadn't wanted to believe it. But now, with Celia confirming it, she had no choice.

A couple of days after this confrontation, Celia's mother came to her home and told her that *she* wanted to talk. She apologized for the alcohol abuse and the neglect and said that she'd been sober now for six months. She admitted that she had suspected Bert was fooling around with Celia and her sister; one night when she was in a drunken rage, she accused him of it. He got mad and stormed out of the house. He never returned, and she had always blamed the girls for that. Now that she was in the AA program, she'd been doing a lot of thinking and knew she needed to make amends with the girls.

Celia has now made contact with her sister after several years of estrangement. She says her sister was as relieved as she to be able to reconnect with her. Both are in the Adult Children of Alcoholics program and struggling to put their lives together.

Esther

Esther decided that she needed a rest from the complications of a relationship, at least for now. She has, however, been learning to enjoy being a part of a family, without thinking of it as her "father's family" and without the guilty feelings of being a traitor to her mother.

Esther and Emily developed a friendship and began to enjoy each other's company very much. Neither had experienced another woman as a close friend before, and it has been a revelation to both of them that they can have such warm, loving feelings for a person of the same sex—feelings that are not sexual but are comfortable and supportive.

Sol, who has never remarried and who has remained in love with

Esther all the years of their separation, has begun to look better and better to her. I'm not willing to make any predictions at this point. However, in my own therapeutic manner, I have encouraged her to reopen the door to their relationship.

Beth Ann

I was a guest at a wedding not long ago, but I felt much more like the mother of the bride than a guest. Try as I do to remain profession-ally detached, some clients defy that, and Beth Ann is one of those. She has made wonderful progress in individual therapy and in group therapy as well. She also attended several meetings of a support group for agoraphobics. At one time she told me she was attending therapy of some sort on a daily basis. She continues to struggle with the negative feelings: the anxiety, insecurity, fear, and guilt that are so crippling. Her husband has been very patient and supportive in many ways, although Beth Ann's disorder is bizarre and difficult for him to understand. She is currently enrolled in a very intense behav-ior modification program at the Phobia Center. We have high hopes for this treatment.

I thought it was very timely and thoughtful of her to plan her wedding so that I'd have a happy ending for my book.

Thanks, Dear Heart.

Emily

Emily is spending quality time with her teenage daughters, and she's spending quality time with herself too: reading, writing poetry, and doing other things she enjoys. She feels happy and peaceful, she says, just living a quiet life. Her mother becomes more dependent on her each year, but Emily seems able to deal with her in a less indulgent manner. I think she has truly forgiven her. She is a lovely person and a delightful lady to know.

Jenny

Jenny returned to the regular classroom in her sophomore year and took her rightful place on the Honor Roll. In her junior year she was captain of her swim team and active in the Arts Club.

Jenny is a senior now, a healthy, beautiful girl. She still possesses a rather quiet nature, but it's a quality that wears well on her. The family relationship has progressed beyond my wildest hopes, and according to Jenny's dad, beyond his as well.

Jenny is making plans for college next year and knows exactly what she wants to do with her life. She plans to become a special education teacher. She has a boyfriend who is a year ahead of her and already in college. Jenny is considering the same school, but her decision has *nothing* to do with him, you understand!

Her parents are not convinced of this fact, but are, very wisely, allowing her to make her own decision. The most difficult job parents have may be that of turning their children's lives over to them to manage.

Melissa

An important part of Melissa's recovery was becoming involved with the group I mentioned earlier. SAFE is a support group dedicated to stopping self-abuse, and between that program and her individual therapy, she is making good progress.

It was an exciting but sad time for us both the day she terminated treatment. She called me once, but when I returned her call she was away on a trip. The next time I called, I was told that she had moved away. I lost contact with her for almost a year, but this past Christmas I got a card saying that she's living in California with her new husband. She says that she is pretty happy and no longer injuring herself, although the compulsion to do so is still with her. She's still active in the SAFE program and in Narcotics Anonymous and says that without all of her self-help work she would not be in recovery. She also says that she's awfully tired of having to constantly work at feeling okay. I've heard this from many others, but the ones I know who are recovering from alcohol or other drug abuse as well as other kinds of obsessive compulsive behaviors are those who "work the program" in AA, NA, or some other self-help organization.

Brian

If ever there was a success story to pull a therapist out of the doldrums (which we often experience), Brian takes the prize. He and Nan have worked very hard to put their marriage back together, going out and enjoying each other for the first time in years. Brian felt better about himself and much of that old anger was gone. I'm not sure when it actually began to dissipate, but my guess is that it was right after his grandmother jumped all over Nan about the way she did Brian's shirts and Brian told her to "butt out."

Nan and Brian had not been in for counseling for several months when Nan called, asking if I would see their eldest daughter. Mindy came to therapy with many problems. She had dropped out of school at fifteen, married at sixteen, mainly to escape the turmoil of the family, and at seventeen found herself with a baby to raise. Her eighteen-year-old husband's maturity level was barely superior to the baby's. The marital relationship was more than dysfunctional; the parenting skills of these two were nonexistent. In spite of her lack of education, Mindy was an intelligent young woman who recognized that she was about to repeat the same dysfunctional pattern in which she had been raised. She agreed that, in order to break the intergenerational cycle of abuse, her work was clearly cut out for her. She did make that commitment, however, and, if she follows through with what we have outlined in therapy, her little boy has a chance for a healthy childhood and a happy life. I have my fingers crossed.

Buddy

For a while, Buddy got his drinking under control and said that he felt healthier than he had in fifteen years. However, his alcoholism had already advanced to the point that he had developed a cirrhotic liver, an irreversible and progressive illness that causes frequent and sudden hemorrhages, jaundiced skin, body swelling, and alcoholic polyneuritis. If he had been able to continue caring for himself, the progress of the illness would have slowed down and he could have lived a fairly good, full life. But such was not the case.

Buddy died just a week after his forty-fourth birthday, and the death certificate proclaimed "acute alcoholism" as the cause of his death. I had been in daily contact with him and, when I was unable to reach him on the phone one evening, I drove to his apartment and found him dead on the floor.

Six weeks earlier, I had forced him to go to the hospital. His liver had failed and the doctor informed him that if he took another drink of alcohol he would die. Even this pronouncement didn't convince him. He continued to drink. Perhaps his disease was at such an advanced stage, that he couldn't stop himself. I don't know.

By the way, I was not really Buddy's therapist, nor was his name "Buddy." His name was Billy Joe Parrish, and he was my husband.

His life story was one of the main reasons I decided to write this book. Although I could not continue to live with him, I shall always continue to love him.

2

RESOURCE
REFERENCE
GUIDE

IX

Digging Into the Past

A Resource Guide to Unblocking Repressed Memory—When You're Ready To Know the Truth

A Variety of Therapeutic Approaches
to Unblocking Repressed Memories
Including Case Histories
compiled by Evan T. Pritchard

Hypnosis and Hypnotherapy—*Sally Flagg Wallis*
Rubenfeld Synergy Method—*Bonnie Jean Garner*
Psychodrama—*Bonnie Jean Garner*
Gestalt Therapy—*Bonnie Jean Garner*
The Affect Bridge—*Dr. Betty Silon*
Empty Chair—*Dr. Betty Silon*
Age Regression—*Dr. Betty Silon*
The Body/Mind Connection (Somatosynthesis),
    —*Dr. Clyde W. Ford*
Past Life Regression—*Dr. Roger Woolger*

Our childhood is like the foundation on which a house is built. If the foundation is cracked, it can cause structural problems in the rest of the house. If the foundation is sound, the house will probably be sound and can be expanded in many ways. The problem with both childhood and foundations is that much of both are deeply buried, and you can't always "go out and fix it yourself." But that doesn't mean it can't be fixed. Sometimes we need to ask for help from someone who is very skilled in a certain area. As one popular bumper sticker proclaims, "It is never too late to have a happy childhood!"

With this in mind, we want to show several different methods, yet to be discussed in this book, by which the effects of child abuse can be treated. Our intent is to show some methods that are being used to dig up buried traumatic memories, although there are many others that may also be successful. When choosing a therapist, you should be sure his or her credentials and references are valid and, where possible, ask a friend to recommend one. You should also trust your intuitive feeling about the therapist. These are very powerful techniques and, in extreme cases, could cause the "roof to cave in" on a severely troubled client.

Each therapist will have developed his or her own techniques, which will be altered to suit the patient's needs, as did each of the therapists quoted here. Because of the many aspects of the recovery process, it can be valuable to work with a therapist who is trained in more than one approach. For the sake of convenience, we have divided some of these techniques into categories, although in practice, such as with Gestalt Therapy, they are often integrated together. Our point is not to be definitive, but to show how different approaches can work in unlocking the door to the troubled past.

Hypnosis and Hypnotherapy
Sally Flagg Wallis

The unconscious mind is receptive to suggestion, and, in fact, is very nonjudgmental and nonlogical; whatever gets through to it, it holds onto as true. Suggestions can be given to it most effectively while the conscious mind, or the judgmental, logical, critical-thinking mind is busied with distraction.

All hypnosis is self-hypnosis; the level of our trance-depth depends upon the individual's willingness to enter into it. Trance is a natural thing to do as anyone can attest who has stared into space for a period of time, daydreamed, or become engaged in one's own reveries while ignoring a speaker. Going into trance, i.e. a hypnotic state, happens automatically and many times a day. Actually, contrary to what our well-intentioned school teachers might say, going "inside" our own thoughts for a while is a very creative thing to do and can be a powerful learning experience.

In contrast, a hypnotic trance can be deliberately induced by oneself or by a trained hypnotherapist. Animals as well as humans can be hypnotized through the use of distraction. Hypnosis is very much like that distracting process, which breaks through resistance or barriers. The aim of hypnosis is not to take away a defense but to make it unnecessary.

Many incidents of sexual abuse occur against young children that go unreported and untreated; when these children become adults, they may be only dimly aware of the past trauma, having stored the experience in the unconscious.

When a victim of abuse becomes motivated to gain greater self-understanding and enters into therapy, he or she may *consciously* desire to know about a trauma that occurred but is not available to their conscious awareness. Hypnotism is one technique that may bridge the gap between unconscious and conscious memory to access those forgotten experiences.

Before plunging in too quickly, however, it is wise to ask the unconscious if it is all right to go back and recall the past experience. If the answer is "yes," then it is all right to proceed. However, if the answer is "no," then perhaps another question can be asked of the unconscious such as, "Is there some part of the past experience that may be too dangerous for me to know, and part of which may be all right for me to know?" Keep in mind that what may not be appropriate to recall now, may open up to us with time, if we are willing.

The natural instinct of every human being is self-protection; the unconscious mind, with its defense and resistance to making some memories "public," is simply demonstrating its capacity to be self-protective of the entire personality.

Case History

Recently, a client came into my office with the presenting problem of marital dissatisfaction; she and her husband of three years could not agree on the amount of physical contact they each wanted. Anna accused him of being a "sex addict," and he was learning that, unless she initiated their sexual activities, it wouldn't work for her. Occasionally, she would say seductive things to him on the phone, then when he came home she would be aloof and cold. During the assessment phase of our counseling sessions, she resisted talking about her feelings regarding their sexual conflicts, but, later in the therapeutic process, she disclosed that she had been sexually assaulted. This report was then clarified to mean that she had been raped by someone unknown to her. As difficult as this was for her to talk about, it further led to an awareness that she had been sexually abused as a young child. As is so typical of sexually and emotionally abused victims who are very young, there is a deprivation of childhood memories. Anna was right on target in this area, as she too had very little recall of any memories of her childhood, pleasant or unpleasant.

Along with her presenting problem, Anna had a serious drinking problem, which she used in a very defiant way to put distance between herself and her husband. Her serious drinking had begun shortly after their marriage, with bouts becoming more frequent with their escalating marital dysfunction.

While in therapy, Anna built up a trust relationship with her therapist; in the counseling process, they agreed that going back to Anna's early childhood memories to access them through hypnosis would be helpful. The goal of retrieving these memories is to reframe them (experience them in a new light) and to bring healing to the wound. As is always the case, whether it be Anna or any other individual, each one of us has an infinite capacity to be creative about how we will heal and recover from old wounds. Anna's trust in her therapist's skill encourages and guides her as she reopens the door to her childhood. With Anna as co-therapist, together they are able to return to past experiences and "grow" Anna up.

Rubenfeld Synergy® Method
Bonnie Jean Garner

Rubenfeld Synergy® Method is an elegant, powerful system of therapy, combining the body/mind healing tools of Moshe Feldenkrais, F.M. Alexander, and Fritz Perls ("Gestalt" therapy), together with the hypnotherapy of Milton Erickson. This gentle technique involves a light, nonintrusive touch, together with verbal expression, imagination, movement, and sound.

It is possible to explore your personal history through this method as well as other transcendent or altered states of being. (Synergy means the action of two or more substances, energies, or techniques to achieve an effect which any one part would not be capable of. However, an older definition of Synergy refers to a combination of human will and divine grace.)

Case History

I would like to first share with you my own experience with this method, my own "case history," so to speak, before I try to present the case histories of others.

One day, at a school for psychotherapy where I was studying, Illana Rubenfeld was conducting a workshop/demonstration on her method. A good friend of mine had just committed suicide, and the school was far away, but in spite of, and perhaps because of, my grief, I called a friend to drive me there anyway. It was not a sensible decision, but it changed the course of my life, both personally and professionally.

The class decided that I would be the demonstration volunteer, since I was in such emotional pain. Fully dressed, except for my shoes, I got on a padded table. It was comfortable. Illana began to gently touch my neck, asking me to let go and notice my feelings. She then stood by my feet and had me imagine energy that could move like a beautiful river from my hips through my feet and beyond. Together we imagined various colors and I noticed how relaxed I was becoming. The class could see how I was holding myself differently, and how deep my breathing had become. With the support of Illana and the whole class, I began to express the deep sorrow I was feeling. Then suddenly a pain shot from my stomach to my jaw.

I decided not to say anything about it, thinking it would pass, but the pain in my jaw persisted for over two weeks, although the session had made me feel much better in other ways. I realized I needed more work done. It was then that I found Joan Lakin, Ph.D., who

was trained in Rubenfeld and psychotherapy, and began private sessions with her.

Joan suggested I take some time to talk and become comfortable
with her, and let her get to know me better too. The pain in my jaw
subsided. It took a few more months for me to trust her, and a few
more before it was time to get back on the table and explore what the
body was trying to tell me.

As I began to let go and explore the "energies" in my body, the
tension in my jaw returned. Joan lightly touched my neck as if to
say, "You are safe now and you can tell me." For some reason I felt
like screaming the word "HELP" yet I was holding my mouth shut
as tightly as possible. Joan suggested I bite on a towel to protect my
teeth. As I did I imagined screaming for help. Then I felt my mouth
open and the memory feeling of gagging and not being able to
breathe returned. I put my hand on my chest and Joan reassuringly
placed her hand lightly on top of mine. I felt like vomiting. Joan asked
me if I wanted to continue. I did.

Although I always remembered some of what had happened to
me as a child, my memory was fuzzy, and I didn't feel much. The
Rubenfeld Method and my trust of Joan enabled me to recall my years
of childhood sexual abuse.

I had been unaware of the powerful connections between past and
present. Suddenly, my life began to make sense. This unknown past
was silently influencing my choices in companions and romance.
Many things that I did or felt I put off to, "that's just the way I am."

No wonder my self-esteem was so low. When a child is mistreated,
deep inside he/she feels there must be something wrong with him/
her. Rediscovering and healing my childhood wounds was pro-
foundly liberating in all aspects of my life, giving me direct access to
my unconscious and its power of recovery.

I was later trained in this method and others. The following are
examples of such methods.

Case History

Lois made her appointment because of a scary, repeating dream.
The dream was brief. She saw baby toys and a large shadowy figure

looming over everything. Instantly she would awaken. Terrified at first, within minutes she would begin sobbing. She couldn't get back to sleep.

"Why would I have such a dream and how come I get like that afterwards?"

"I'm not sure, Lois. Are you willing to tell me about your life, past and present?"

Knowing more was very important to Lois. The choice was hers every step of the way.

What Lois revealed was, in many ways, a wonderful childhood. There was no alcoholism, no overt family violence, few financial problems. It was stable.

But Lois always disliked her father. He was always complaining of some illness or another. She grew sick herself of hearing his ongoing complaints and fears. "Hypochondriac!" she thought.

As an adult, Lois was successful and independent. She had never married and was not dating at this time. She had begun to gain some weight and noticed that she felt like drinking, which was unusual.

Through our weekly explorations, Lois discovered that emotionally she took care of her mother. She always had. In fact, Lois was a great "caretaker." Through suggested reading, Lois began to see that, although her family did not fit the mold of an alcoholic family, they were dysfunctional. Her one brother did not get along with the father either. He moved far away and had very little contact with either parent.

As comfort, trust, and awareness deepened through weekly sessions, I introduced the idea of possibly using the Rubenfeld Synergy Method to uncover more information.

Lois, fully clothed, except for her shoes, lay face up on a padded RSM table. Although we had intended to work directly with the dream images, this method invites a journey into the unconscious. Lois was curious and willing to listen and stay open to the process. She trusted that her unconscious would open whatever doors were useful to her now.

As Lois relaxed and attended to her body feelings and the simultaneous images that kept appearing within her, she felt a "knot" tighten in her stomach. "A knot," I said, "like in 'not this?'"

"Yes," she said, "like in 'not this.'"

I invited her to feel the knot and repeat the words "not this" and see what happens. As the tension in her stomach began to increase, and she took a deep breath and said, "I wish I could get this out."

"Yes, I know you do," I replied. Lois began sobbing quietly, "Somebody hurt me, Bonnie. (Pause) I can feel it and I feel confused," she said.

For support, I lightly set my hand on hers upon her stomach.

"Are you in touch with the pain and confusion here?" I asked.

"Yes," she cried, "and now my jaw is shaking."

"Hmm, Lois. See if you can allow that shaking to happen. That is the energy of some of the feelings you have been holding back. I noticed your shoulders are hunching up towards your neck."

"Yeah."

"Lois, just allow your body to do what it needs to right now, and we can listen to what it is saying."

As she did, it became obvious to her that she was feeling fear.

"Who is scaring you?" I asked.

"Oh, my God, it's my father. I keep seeing him in my mind and he is big and the room is sort of dark and shadowy." (Pause) Her body tightened more. "No, nooo, no, nooo, nooo," she cried.

"Lois, I am right here with you," I said as I repositioned my hands near her neck and head. "Can you say what is going on?"

"Oh, God, Bonnie, I can feel him and see him touching me . . . (crying) . . . I have really always hated him, but I've never known why . . . (crying) . . . how could he? . . . (Crying).

Follow Up

Over the course of many sessions, some of her memory returned. She remembered that at nine years old she told her mother she did not want her father to babysit for her anymore. Her mother never asked her why, but her father also never babysat alone for her again. She asked her mother if she remembered that incident. Her mother could not remember why she made the decision but did say, "I think your father started to get sick a lot then and for his health I did not ask him to watch you kids. I stopped going to PTA and other places without him."

The unfoldment and healing process continued for Lois, clarifying her current attitudes and behaviors concerning her body, men, and sex. She is facing many challenges today and charting her own course in her healing as well as in her life. Lois also recognized a relationship between these memories (in the form of dreams) returning and her desire to have a committed relationship. About two months before these dreams began recurring, she decided that she did want marriage and a family.

Today she is grateful for her knowing the truth, as it has helped her learn how to feel and be safer in this world. She is currently dating, and they are considering a future together.

Psychodrama
Bonnie Jean Garner

Psychodrama is a creative form of therapy. When used with a group, it provides support, exploration, creativity, spontaneity, and learning. The principal elements are: the main character—who wishes to explore some aspect of the unconscious or life as a whole; the therapist—who directs and guides the action, sets the stage, and supports the main character; and the imagination, memory, and concerns of the group. Group participants who are willing, play roles for each other. From the roles and the relationships, clients can express, explore, or change their story.

In the psychodynamic process, the group offers to role-play past, present, or future life situations for each other. Afterwards, everyone shares how they related to what occurred, both from their role and from their own life. Active re-enactment to the point of memory loss can sometimes induce spontaneous memory recall. Again this is best to occur and most likely to occur in a trusted and safe group environment. There are many questions to be answered after memory returns. It is valuable to have a trained and trusted therapeutic relationship in which to discover your own answers. It is a highly recommended method of recovery and discovery for members of dysfunctional families. However, the choices are many and varied.

Case History

Linda had nightmares from time to time. They were almost always the same. She was just about to be raped and she would awaken.

Ever since she was young, she had shooting pains in her body. Her parents and everyone else passed them off as "growing pains." At twenty-nine, Linda was still having them from time to time. Whenever she stayed at a friend's house, or even sometimes at home, for just a brief moment she would imagine that someone could shoot her or break down the door and get her. It was fleeting, and something she had never spoken about. Linda did not realize that she had forgotten much of her childhood. When cousins and friends talked and laughed about the past, she enjoyed the conversations. She laughed and listened. Slowly it dawned on her that she never contributed to them.

Linda turned to counseling during the breakup of a five-year relationship. "Somewhere inside of me, something says, 'Why couldn't I read the writing on the wall? He was a rat to his last girlfriend. He cheated on her.' I wanted to believe that he did what he did to her because she was who she was . . . and . . . that he would never treat me that way. The worst thing is that I'm scared to trust my own judgment now, and without that, I feel lost. . . ."

At twenty-nine, Linda could not figure out why she sometimes felt that she would never get married. It seemed simple enough for everyone else but her.

Linda attended weekly private sessions with me. Most of the time was spent sorting through her feelings. She began to explore her childhood a bit. Because there was alcoholism in her family, Linda was willing to attend ACOA meetings. I invited her to attend an ongoing monthly intensive therapeutic group.

One of the techniques I used with the group was the "psychodynamic" process.

Linda liked the people in the group. After a while, Linda asked the group to help her in re-enacting an event at a family picnic. She was about ten years old. She remembered taking a ride with her brother's older friends. She knew they drove down a back road. They stopped the pickup truck and that was about all she recalled. This event unnerved her. Linda was beginning to suspect that her dreams, fleeting fears, and memory loss might all be related.

As the group members role-played this scene, Linda started to cry. She grabbed my hand and dropped to the floor. She began to recall how terrified she was that day. These older boys touched her and teased her. They did not take her clothes off or rape her. They did threaten her that if she ever told anyone, even her older brother, they would "get" her. Part of Linda had remained paralyzed with fear all these years. The big fear is "not telling" because abuse is so often followed by punishments or threats not to tell. Even after "telling," adult survivors of child abuse often have fear of punishment.

The group gathered in a circle around Linda. I asked her to peek out and look around at the group. She saw the softness in the eyes of the group members.

"How can this group help you right now, Linda?" I asked.

Through her tears she said, "Tell me I am safe now and that nothing's going to happen to me, because I've "told.""

The group reassured her.

Over the next few months Linda continued to express the many different feelings surrounding this event. The group role-played this again and again with Linda. Each time they changed the story, encouraging Linda to tell the older boys off and to express her fears and anger.

Sometimes Linda would have someone else play her as a little girl. In doing this, Linda could step into the re-enactment to protect herself and soothe the frightened child within.

Follow Up

With the combination of private sessions, ACOA, and this group process, Linda was very pleased with her personal growth. She gained more confidence in herself and her capacity to speak out. Unlocking her memory and being able to process it so fully was crucial to her recovery.

And yes, those nightmares are gone.

Gestalt Therapy
Bonnie Jean Garner

One of the basic concepts in Gestalt is our need to complete experiences—to say what we could not say, express the feelings of that moment, or take the action we could not take then. Once this is completed we are freer and have greater energy to deal with our lives. This is done in the safety of this technique, allowing the past and present to come into harmony.

Case History

Maria called me after watching a popular television talk show on the topic of "men who cheat on their wives." I was the first therapist she had ever spoken to. Maria had known about her husband's "flings." Although they hurt, she wanted her marriage. As the years went by, it became harder for Maria to pretend everything was fine. She was unhappy and felt like she was in a rut, unable to do anything good for herself or to have fun. The show made the point that whatever you do, "get yourself emotional support!"

In session, Maria revealed that her father left her home when she was eleven years old. She did not remember much before then, except that she was told her parents fought a lot. Her father returned to live with the family again when Maria was thirteen, and at that time, she learned she had a half brother . . . somewhere.

Maria made the connection between her tolerance towards her husband and her love of her father. She was always more of a "Daddy's Girl," favoring her father's attention over her mother's. As sessions progressed, it became clear that in some ways her mother had been abusive to Maria. Through Rubenfeld Synergy Method, some of her early memory returned. Maria had repressed unpleasant memories of her mother chasing her around the house, threatening to kill her, and hitting her with a belt. Apparently, this happened quite a bit, and she remembered that many of her parents' arguments were over how to take care of her.

What Maria wondered was, "How did I as a kid continue on in my life with all that stuff happening? How was I able to go on and date, have fun, play sports, have friends?"

Maria felt as if some part of her, some vital part, was gone —lost— maybe forever. This seemed to tie in directly with her difficulties taking care of herself today, or standing up to others, no matter what anyone, including her husband, did.

She felt strongly that if she could get that "spark" back, she could continue to make changes in herself and in the quality of her life.

"Who knows," she said, "maybe I could even confront my husband?"

This was a wonderful opportunity to utilize a technique in Gestalt therapy called, "The Empty Chair." Like all of the therapies being shared here with you, Gestalt is a creative and fascinating therapeutic intervention. The theory of Gestalt is far too encompassing to write about here, and the varieties of applications too far reaching for the purpose of this case study. This technique invites, among other things, clarity through exploration of the past in the present moment. I explained to Maria that we would place an empty chair across from her, and she was to imagine herself sitting in it, a child again. Then she could begin a dialogue with this part of herself.

Maria was willing to begin.

"How does the little Maria look?" I asked.

"Hmmm . . . I can imagine her like some of the pictures I've seen of myself at about fifteen years old . . . I didn't think I would imagine myself that old. . . ."

"That's okay, Maria. What would you like to ask her or say to her now? You can begin, if you like, by telling her you are from her future."

"This feels a little weird, but here goes . . . Maria, I can see you there, you look so energetic. I am you . . . grown up . . . but there is something you have . . . something I lost or have at least forgotten. [Maria's eyes begin to fill up with tears.] What, what could you have that I have forgotten?"

I instructed Maria to change seats and, as she did so, to allow herself to relax into the fifteen-year-old Maria who is still part of her today.

Maria sat on the empty chair. She closed her eyes. After a moment, I said to her, "Maria, can you tell us about yourself from this place? Meanwhile, let the answer to the question you have been asking formulate now."

"Well, I'm fifteen, and I like to have fun. I know a lot of stuff that you [talking back to the chair where the older Maria had been sitting] have forgotten. I want you to remember all of it because it all made me strong. Why have you forgotten me?"

I cue silently for Maria to switch chairs and answer this question.

"Made me strong? Well, maybe you're right. You look stronger than I feel and sitting there I felt stronger. I don't know why I forgot you, except that I got busy with life, and. . . ."

I suggested that adult Maria start slowly with one thing at a time.

Perhaps for this first session she should ask this part what she needs to remember that would be useful in her recovery. Maria did so. Then switching seats again, she learned a powerful secret from her child-self.

"I have this secret deal with God, ever since I'm little. No matter how bad it gets, no matter how hurt I feel, I go to sleep and wake up saying two prayers. I agree with God, 'I'll give you my hurt and love, and you give me my life and love.'

Maria began in a sing-song voice to recite two prayers.

When she was done, she was glowing. She looked so happy. I asked her to switch. When she did, she looked a little surprised. "What's going on for you?" I asked.

"I . . . I can't believe that I would have forgotten that!"

"Maria," I asked, "would you be willing to recite the two prayers from this place (the adult Maria)?"

She nodded and as she began to do so, tears and laughter began to flow from her. "I want to scoop that part of me up for a great big hug!!"

I handed her a pillow and said, "Let this be the energy of that part, hug her, tell her whatever you need to, and then imagine taking the energy and awareness inside of you to integrate peacefully now.

Maria was quiet and withdrew inside herself for a few moments. Then she smiled at me and put the pillow down.

"There is more to do and more to remember, but I'm not so afraid now. Somehow I just feel stronger."

Follow Up

Maria continued with sessions, occasionally using this technique along with others. Her spirituality helped her to get more honest, first with herself and then with her husband. He agreed to enter counseling with her, and they are trying to work things out. Her hurtful childhood set the stage for this kind of challenge, and she realizes now that she has many more choices and many more resources than she has ever had before.

The Affect Bridge
Dr. Betty Silon

The affect bridge can be used when we are under hypnosis and there are feelings present, such as fear, mistrust, or confusion, or of physical sensations, such as sharp pains or choking. If these sensations relate directly to the problems we are dealing with right now, it can be a way to help us make an association from the present to the past, so that we regress and retrieve vague or repressed memories which are affecting our present life condition. When we focus on the feeling or sensation connected to the problem, and intensify it, we create a memory bridge that links us to a past situation that produced a similar effect.

Early recollections reveal the source of our present life style attitudes, patterns, and rules that are consistent with our behavior. The affect bridge can assist us to remove or gain control over our symptoms and change our attitude, awareness, and behavior.

Case History

Kathy initially entered hypnotherapy for weight loss and to work on her relationships with men. She was 46 years old, a special education teacher, and had been divorced for ten years. She had most of the responsibility for raising her two adolescent children, who became the focus of her life. Kathy was a very pleasant, jolly, but passive, childlike, and co-dependent individual. She had been psychologically abused as a child by her manipulative, controlling, and obsessive mother, and sexually assaulted by her teen-age brother when she was 12 years of age.

It was during her marriage to a very controlling and rigid man, whom she served and lived in fear of displeasing, that she developed a compulsive eating disorder and gained a great deal of weight. As a child, her mother had set limits on what she would eat, and in her marriage her husband attempted to do the same. The more she used food to nurture herself, the more distant he became.

Since her divorce she has not been able to have a satisfying relationship with a man. Those men she has been involved with have used her and demeaned her sexually. Before she came to see me, she had spent a year in California with Robert. He manipulated her into believing he was interested in a relationship with her, but after several months he showed signs of being more interested in her 14-year-old daughter. Kathy was so naive and in need of love and attention that she did not understand that she had placed her daughter at risk sexually.

As Robert began to lavish attention on her daughter, Kathy and her daughter became rivals. While Kathy was working, Robert would take her daughter on trips. Kathy found herself alone more and more and finally decided to return home with her daughter. In his letters Robert declared his love for the daughter, which created a great deal of terror and panic in Kathy for her daughter's safety, as well as jealousy and anger towards her for being the object of Robert's affections. It was at this point that Kathy came to see me, and we worked together to find out how she had become a chronic victim. First, we sorted out her feelings toward herself, Robert, and her daughter. As we progressed in therapy, she was able to speak to her daughter and learn she had not been sexually assaulted by Robert, but that both she and her daughter had been emotionally raped. She was able to take a stand with Robert and cut off all communication with him. As Kathy asserted herself, her daughter expressed her anger and disgust with Robert and sent back his letters and gifts.

It was then we began the journey back to Kathy's past and her relationship with her mother. She was the youngest of three children in a very prominent mid-western family. Her father was a judge, who was more a playmate than parent. He left the child-rearing to mother, who ran a boarding school and was a respected teacher and caretaker of children.

Kathy only remembers being touched when she was being fed or dressed. Mother was a caretaker, who had emotionally neglected and deprived her children of affection, touching, and attention. Mother relentlessly made all the decisions, offering no alternatives. She was always watching or spying on the children and even drilled peep-holes throughout the house to ensure good behavior. Even after it was discovered that Kathy's brother was sexually molesting her, it was kept a family secret and never discussed with Kathy.

Kathy would bring to our sessions her family pictures and the baby book in which her mother recorded Kathy's growth. In the book, her mother wrote about how good and pleasant Kathy was as an infant. She was so proud of how she could keep Kathy outside in a bassinet for hours and hours, and not even have to check on her. When it would rain or snow her mother would put her in a room in the bassinet and keep the windows open so the child would get air. Kathy was shocked with disbelief that a mother could neglect a child for such long periods of time.

In therapy, Kathy came to realize that she was an inconvenience, interfering with her mother's duties at her school, which always came first, as did the needs of her mother's students. Kathy grew up doing everything possible to be a good girl and please her mother, for she knew if she did not she would have the few privileges she had taken away from her.

Kathy, a very social, outgoing child, sought attention from anyone who would talk to her. She was made to spend a great deal of time alone playing in her room. She was put to bed very early and warned never to leave her bed. She would lie there using her imagination to entertain herself.

During one of our first hypnotherapy sessions, Kathy regressed to a night in her room when she was seven years old. She became focused on the lights of trucks, for, as they would pass her window, they would shine their lights on her walls, creating rectangular shapes, which she would hypnotically count. This game was another creative means of comforting and nurturing herself while imprisoned in her room. During this session, Kathy put her hands and arms behind her back, which pushed her stomach out, making her look like a Buddha.

In later sessions, whenever Kathy would begin to feel angry, she would repress the emotion, fidget in her chair, and place her arms behind her back, appearing to be in a dissociated state. I confronted her with this observation, but she denied there could be any connection to her emotions. The reason she did this, she said, was that the chair in my office was not comfortable. "The arms were not big enough."

During a session, when Kathy was sitting with her arms behind her back and getting in touch with her anger, I suggested that we do hypnotherapy. During the trance induction, her eyes remained open, and as they would blink, she would go deeper into trance. I asked her to become aware of any feelings or sensations she was having and to let those sensations or feelings act as a bridge ("affect bridge") to a time in the past when she was under six years old. She said she was experiencing tension in her stomach. I asked her to intensify her awareness of that tension and to find an early recollection where she experienced the same feelings or sensations.

Kathy recalled a time when she was between four and five years old, when she went into the kitchen. The pantry door, which held, among other things, yardsticks, was open. She could smell the furniture wax and turpentine from the cleaning rags that her mother collected and stored in the pantry. She became tense and terrified, for her mother was in the kitchen and began hitting her with a yardstick. She placed her hands behind her back to protect her bottom. Suddenly she said, "Now I know why she would hit me whenever I went into the kitchen. She was in there sneaking food and didn't want anyone to see her."

We talked for a while about her fear of her mother and the kitchen, and how helpless she felt when she was being struck. Still in a trance and discussing her emotions, Kathy spontaneously regressed to a time when she was under 1½ years old, sitting in her feeding table, which was in the same location in the kitchen where she was hit with the yardstick. Her feeding table was very high, which was frightening, and the feeding tray was hurting her, as it was braced up against her body to prevent her from moving. Her hands and arms were tied behind her back with her bib, and her legs were restrained. She so wanted to pick up the spoon on her tray to feed herself. She wanted to kick her legs and wave her arms, but the only part of herself she could move were the curls on top of her head, which she could bob around.

A smile was on her face as she patiently sat waiting to be fed by her mother who was at the sink preparing food. Kathy described her longing for her mother to turn around and pay attention to her, so she kept smiling, holding onto that hope. As she shared this significant, early memory, Kathy sounded and looked like a young, wounded child and began to cry.

She would do anything to be noticed, so she chose to be "forever pleasant and patient." Kathy wept for the wounded child within who was constrained and controlled by a mother who had to always be appeased and still was not nurturing.

In looking back, Kathy came to realize that she was not confined to her chair for hours to be fed, but was there to keep her from bothering her mother while she attended to business matters for the school. Her mother did not allow Kathy to feed herself or touch her food, for fear of staining her dress. Kathy became aware that she was not hungry for food, but hungry for attention from her mother.

It was then I asked Kathy if she would like to change the past and move from the position of victim to survivor, to free herself from mother's control. She agreed, and we utilized a psychodramatic method called The Empty Chair technique.

Empty Chair

Dr. Betty Silon

As explained earlier, the empty chair is a role-playing technique used in psychodrama and Gestalt therapy. It is performed by the main character without the help of supporting "actors," so that we interact with an imagined live or dead person with whom we are emotionally involved. The empty chair (or chairs) may also represent another part of the self, a skill, a concept, or an inanimate object. It helps us deal with painful confrontations and can be used to face feelings or situations one may otherwise avoid or deny, or to rehearse a confrontation before we have to face it in reality. With the use of monologues and role-reversals, we can change roles as we change seats, helped by the therapist, who acts as director. This can also be done using hypnosis.

Case History—(continued)

Kathy, while still in trance, expressed the pain and learned helplessness of the wounded child. I suggested that she move to the empty chair and be an adult Kathy, who would be present to encourage and protect the vulnerable child. It was inconceivable even for the adult Kathy to find a solution, so that little Kathy could get mother's attention and get out of the feeding table. She kept shouting, "Mother would never allow that, Mother would never allow that, she would get mad at me."

I next asked Kathy to use the creative part of herself to bring forth an inner guide who could help her attain a degree of freedom. She brought Winky, an imaginary animal her father had introduced her to in a game. Winky sat in the empty chair for a moment and then silently and fervently untied Kathy's restraints. Together they ran outside and freely danced and played.

In processing the therapeutic session, Kathy acknowledged how powerless she felt in relationship to her mother and food. So much so that the only means she could devise to free herself from the feeding table was through her imagination, for mother could not see Winky release her from her prison. Developmentally, Kathy is frozen at a very early stage in life. As a co-dependent, she has not developed the ability to be psychologically autonomous, and she allows others to have power over her feelings and reactions.

Follow Up

Kathy is now conscious of the lengths she has gone to please and appease her mother, men, and her children throughout her life. She is also aware that when she does not get nurturing and attention, she uses food as a substitute, eating when she is not hungry. Kathy is still in therapy and has begun to nurture and assert herself, by setting limits with herself and others. We have also begun to use hypnosis for weight loss.

Age Regression
Dr. Betty Silon

In age regression—usually under hypnosis—we alter our behavior and return to a former age and actually relive the past experience of being the small child to whom we have age-regressed. The event is perceived through the eyes of a child, as are the emotions, how one speaks and behaves. Reliving the past while in the present is actually a form of "dissociation" but has a therapeutic effect. "Dissociation" is an altered state of awareness used as a survival tool during childhood sexual trauma, as well as in later years, in order to protect ourselves from further abuse, imagined or real.

Age regression occurs not only in hypnotic trance, but whenever we recall an event or repressed memory associated with a particular age or several ages. It can occur spontaneously, such as when we look through a photograph album or yearbook.

Case History

Jackie is a thirty-five year old mother of four children, ranging in age from six months to nineteen years old. She is an attractive, wide-eyed, hypervigilant, hysterical, sensitive, and creative woman who has been at different times anorexic, has had TMJ, and has a dissociative disorder. She came to see me because she was experiencing agoraphobia (fear of open spaces). I have seen Jackie both in individual and group therapy for almost two years.

Jackie, a middle child of three, had been chronically sexually assaulted by her father since the age of six. She ran away from home to live with her boyfriend's family when she was fifteen years old and married him when she was seventeen, while pregnant with their first child, a daughter. Jackie periodically left her husband, but came back, for he was the only loving and stable force in her life. There is a part of Jackie who is always running.

Through the years, she became estranged from her family. Although she feared her father, who became mentally ill, she loved and protected him, keeping the secret of the abuse. It was not until her mid-twenties that she finally told her dependent, passive mother, who denied knowing anything about the abuse. She admitted that she too was afraid of her husband, who she enabled to victimize the entire family. Jackie lost touch with her sister, who also was sexually abused by the father. Neither sister knew about the other's abuse until six years ago. Jackie became the rescuer of her younger brother, who drifted from crisis to crisis.

She became a crisis counselor in the church. Although Jackie was excellent at rescuing others, it was also a way for her to lose herself and hide her shame. She trusted no one, creating a false self to cover her isolation and woundedness, which worked until she began having panic attacks and could not go anywhere by herself, resulting in her becoming agoraphobic.

When Jackie first came into individual therapy, she talked of sexual abuse, but as if she were talking of someone else. She had a great deal of anticipatory anxiety, fearing that she would remember things that would make her lose control even more than she already had. Jackie had no memory of anything before age eleven.

Jackie also entered group therapy with other agoraphobics and would have panic attacks each time she came to the group. In time, Jackie and I developed a therapeutic rapport, and she agreed to cooperate in hypnotherapy. During one of our individual sessions, I used age regression to assist Jackie in retrieving repressed early memories about her abuse. When Jackie regressed to age eight she became very panicky, so I asked her to go back to age five. Life then was good and peaceful, a time of innocence.

We moved slowly up through the years and came again to eight years old. Jackie again became very anxious, but began to imagine herself trapped in her own room, which she described in detail. No one was home but her dad, who was in his room. She was terrified that he would call her to come there to take care of him, for he would tell her he was ill. She knew that she would have to masturbate him so he would feel better. He would also tell her to not tell anyone he was sick, for he did not want Jackie's mother to worry. Jackie during earlier times felt important that she was his rescuer; but, now that she was eight, she was beginning to realize that he was not really sick, but only pretending, and that this was wrong.

While still in trance, I asked Jackie if she trusted herself as an adult to go into the house to protect that part of her who was a wounded child. The adult Jackie agreed and brought young Jackie out of the house, which was a freeing experience. Jackie said, "It felt so different to have someone take care of me." The adult Jackie held and nurtured the wounded child within and sang her a lullaby. "I love you so much . . . I'm thankful to have you as part of myself."

Jackie felt a "union" of the needy child and the loving mother. I asked Jackie, the adult, if she would take little Jackie into the house and confront her mother for leaving her alone. She agreed and told her mother to never leave her alone with dad, for he did bad things.

Jackie said she was having angry feelings about her dad. I asked if she would be willing to confront him psychodramatically. She agreed but could not say a word. It was as if she were still eight years old, trapped in her room waiting for him to call her, alone and without support.

I asked Jackie to move to an empty chair across the room and told her, "You are Jackie, a wife and mother of four." As she walked across the room, her demeanor changed and she became more confident. I asked Jackie to choose another group member to play her wounded child. When Jackie looked at her vulnerable self, she was filled with compassion and a new-found courage. Another chair was placed in the center of the group, which was to hold Jackie's father. Jackie went through a range of emotion, but she was finally able to release her anger and tell him that what he did was wrong and unfair, and that he should have protected her.

When Jackie would reverse roles with her father, she experienced his denial and pain, for he too had been sexually abused as a child. Jackie eventually felt stronger than him and was able to perceive his weakness. As a child she was the weak one, and he was strong. She knew that when he called she had to go. He was her father, and she loved him. She also knew that the caring part of her believed she was truly helping him, all of which confused her and gave him power over her.

Jackie's defense against the pain of her woundedness was to split herself into good and bad. She also split her dad into good and bad father, for no matter how bad he was, she still loved the idealized father she created. As Jackie began to feel a sense of "union" again, she was able to tell him that she always worried about whether she could be a good parent, and, in a burst of anger, said, "You did not know the meaning of the word father!"

The group cheered and supported Jackie's courage to confront and separate from her abuser, and to stop running through life confused, sometimes a victim, and at other times the abuser of herself, as well as the rescuer of others. Jackie left therapy for a while but has recently returned, for she knows she cannot keep running from healing herself and resolving other issues in her life.

The Body/Mind Connection (Somatosynthesis)
Dr. Clyde W. Ford

Abuse always involves the human body. In sexual abuse where the body is the object of abuse, this is self-evident. But the body is also involved in emotional abuse as well. Emotional abuse, like physical and sexual abuse, involves inappropriate touch. While touch is used inappropriately in sexual abuse, in emotional abuse it is inappropriately withheld. Lack of physical contact is at the heart of the neglect and abandonment that occur with abuse.

There are more complex reasons why the body is always involved in abuse. Children are often abused during sensitive periods when physical and psychological development are occurring simultaneously. At such crucial times, violating the body leaves psychological wounds, while violating the psyche leaves physical wounds.

Physical or sexual abuse, particularly during the time when a very young child is learning that it exists apart from its mother, can keep the child from developing clear boundaries of his or her own identity—boundaries that assist the formation of a healthy ego. This sets the stage for the eventual emergence of a personality disorder described as "borderline."

I have often seen a similar process happen in young women at puberty—another crucial juncture of physical/psychological development. In these cases, a young woman's emerging sexuality is threatened in some way. This usually involves the development of the breasts, inappropriate remarks by family members, fondling or other sexual abuse, or even social stigmas associated with the rapid sexual development of pubescent woman.

Regardless of the cause, the result is that physical development is suppressed. Much later in life, women have remembered "stooping over" to hide the development of their breasts or "slouching" because they were told they were too tall. These postural changes interfered with normal growth and development. They were scars from abuse and are carried by the body for many years after.

As a clinician trained to treat physical disorders, I am naturally interested in the way our bodies store and reveal the insults that have been hurled at us throughout life. Through a process I term somatosynthesis, I have effectively used touch to recall and work through the emotional memories of the body. The somatosynthesis process is based on the importance of the body (soma) in synthesizing physical and psychological experience.

The somatosynthesis process has four basic steps:

1. Touch is used to heighten a person's awareness of a given area of the body.

2. The individual is asked to "map" the area of the physical body to a psychological issue or event.

3. Touch is used to facilitate the emergence of the emotions and feelings surrounding this event.

4. Touch is used to facilitate a resolution of the emotions and feelings surrounding this event.

Case History

In the three years I had seen Jennifer as a patient, there was no mention of childhood sexual abuse. She was a forty-two-year-old woman who owned a popular local restaurant. Jennifer and her husband were also seeing a local psychotherapist for a variety of marital problems.

Periodically she would make an appointment with me complaining of lower back pain, which she always attributed to the demands of her job. At one such appointment Jennifer informed me that she was also having pain further up her spine. I gently supported Jennifer's body with one hand underneath her back and the other hand resting lightly on her diaphragm. As I did she began to cough violently and she complained of feeling nauseated. "I want to cough it up," she said, "and get it out of my body."

Jennifer's words were fraught with symbolic meaning, and her cough was one that I have encountered in many survivors of sexual abuse. I asked what it was she felt needed to come out, but she said she was not sure. However, she continued to cough.

I now used both hands to gently pump her stomach as though I were helping to bring up and out whatever was there. Unsure whether she would really vomit, I gave her a tissue, asked her to turn on her stomach and hang her head over my treatment table. I used a similar pumping action along her spine while she continued to cough and heave. This went on for nearly 20 minutes although she never really vomited. At the end of this ordeal, Jennifer was crying, shaking, and visibly upset.

"What happened," she demanded to know.

"I'm not really sure," I informed her. "Your body felt like it was in the midst of a very unpleasant experience."

Over the next several sessions a similar pattern emerged. We were constantly simulating the removal of things from Jennifer's body: objects in her abdomen and lower back, foul liquid that she needed to vomit, or uneasy feelings that were lodged in various parts of her body.

Only after this symbolic removal was Jennifer able to examine what caused these objects to be lodged in her. At one session she spoke about seeing a house with a little girl inside. The little girl was very upset and she was afraid to speak with anyone. We found a safe place for Jennifer to take the little girl and speak with her about why she was so upset.

Through Jennifer's inner child we learned about Jennifer being fondled by her father and uncle from childhood through her teen-age years. It was the first time Jennifer had spoken to anyone about this history of sexual abuse. Over the next sessions, more of Jennifer's feelings surfaced. Rage, shame, pain, and other emotions often first emerged as objects located within her body. We could always figure out a way of using touch to simulate the removal of these objects. Once they were removed, Jennifer could experience and release the underlying emotions. In this way, touch became a powerful ally in Jennifer's recovery from abuse.

Our bodies are reservoirs for memories too painful for our conscious mind. Psychological intervention alone holds no guarantee of recovering these deeply buried memories. Often the body's memories must be accessed directly, and touch is itself a therapeutic language for unlocking and resolving embodied emotions. But our bodies store more than just the pain, anger, and shame of abuse. Our bodies also store the comfort, joy, and hope of recovery. Through touch we can access these varied memories and help abuse survivors reclaim those parts of themselves that were lost or taken away. This is the essence of the somatosynthesis process.

Past Life Regression
Dr. Roger Woolger

Past life regression therapy is a therapeutic technique that superficially resembles hypnotic age regression but which also draws strongly from both guided imagery practices such as Carl Jung's "ac-

tive imagination" and J.L. Moreno's psychodrama. Like hypnotic regression, the patient is guided back to and encouraged to relive traumatic scenes from the past that have been lost to consciousness. But
instead of being regressed to the patient's current childhood, a strong
suggestion is given that he or she go back to a "previous life" in
which the trauma originated.

What is remarkable about this technique, which was first used at
the turn of the century by the French hypnotist Colonel de Rochas,
is that the patient does not need to believe in reincarnation or past
lives for it to be effective. He or she simply relives a distressing scene
from some other historical time frame, as if it were real and very
much in a different historical persona and a different body image.
The therapeutic effect of the reliving of the "past-life" trauma—acci-
dent, abandonment, violent death, rape, betrayal, etc.—is similar to
that of current life traumas and in fact directly reflects many of them.
The reliving is like a fictional psychodrama that leads, as Moreno
wished, to an intense cathartic release of blocked feelings, whether
fear, grief, rage, or guilt.

Past life regression has been used very effectively in working with
victims of current-life child sexual abuse because it effectively dis-
places the trauma into a totally different psychological frame in the
imagined or remembered past. Where many patients may have difficulty recalling and releasing fears about an incident with a living
parent or known abuser, past life regression seems to free up the
unconscious to release both physical details and emotional aspects
of the abuse that were otherwise blocked. Often, the effect of reliving
the "past-life" abuse is that the patient—often in the same session—
slips into the current life abuse scenario to find him- or herself spontaneously saying the very same words or manifesting similar emotional and bodily reactions such as disgust, terror, physical writhing,
muscular rigidity, and so on.

The experience of a growing number of therapists is that past life
regression is a powerful tool for, among other issues, working
through childhood abuse scenarios. Most of the time, therapists have
found it unnecessary to even raise the question of reincarnation but
may simply suggest something like "just let a story emerge from the
unconscious that might be the origin of your feelings, as though it
happened in another time and place."

Continued encounters with "past-life" memories begin to raise in many people's minds the issue of whether they are real memories from the past and not just fantasies. For, in fact, past-life memories are extremely realistic and there is no question that young children can recall them without having any idea what they are about. For the most part they remain dormant, but because of the magnetic power of a complex, the patient attracts situations where these buried stories will be either imaginarily or physically replayed. It often seems as if the current life abuse is in fact part of a deep repetition compulsion, to use Freud's term, or a condition that has "fatalistic" or even "karmic" resonances to it. Even though the therapist may meticulously avoid giving such suggestions, certain patients frequently report "recognizing" their abuser from a previous life but see them also as a child or a woman they had themselves abused in yet another past life. It can be quite sobering for them to discover in these seeming past lives that both abuser and abused have been through it all before and often with the roles reversed. At such times, the idea of karma—that past life actions precondition the circumstances and patterns of the present—seems inescapable.

Note: In the early days of psychoanalysis, Sigmund Freud was deeply confused as to whether adult hysteria arose from actual childhood sexual abuse or from infantile sexual fantasies of incest. Unable to believe that *all* his clients had been sexually abused, Freud postulated instead a powerful universal infantile fantasy component that he dubbed the Oedipus complex. Unfortunately this drew attention away from actual sexual abuse and may have seriously retarded investigation into its incidence by many decades. Jeffrey M. Masson discusses this in his book *The Assault on Truth: Freud's Suppression of the Seduction Theory*.

From the perspective of our current knowledge of past-life regression, it seems possible that Freud was misled by his adult patients' garbled recall of a mixture of both current life abuse and past life residues of abuse that had become fused in their unconscious memory. In addition, there may of course, have been cases where there was no childhood abuse at all but a relatively innocuous stimulus—a military uniform, the sound of a scream for example—that triggered a past life memory in the child's deep unconscious. Many past life therapists now believe that such residues are also the stuff of night terrors.

Case History

Melinda had consulted several therapists about her failure to form close relationships with men and her near frigidity when it came to sexual contact. For a period she had been in a lesbian relationship, which helped her somewhat, because her lover wanted companionship more than physical contact. Yet the root issue remained untouched. She reported a clear memory of sexual molestation at eleven years. A twelve-year-old boy from the neighborhood had enticed her into a disused garage and had fondled her genitally, though he had not attempted penetration. Her retelling of the story was cold and detached; she seemed to hold herself clenched as she told it. Apparently she had talked about this event many times with her previous therapists and, though she had also beaten out her rage on pillows and mattresses, part of her was still holding unfinished anger.

When I invited her to lie down on a mattress to relive the event, her clenching became even more pronounced:

"I don't want to do this," she says, with markedly more anger in her voice now.

"Lie down anyway and keep repeating that phrase to whoever it applies to," I urge gently.

With her eyes closed, the following monologue emerges with very little prompting from me other than to direct her to repeat certain phrases and to exaggerate her bodily posture:

"I don't want to do this. I don't want to do this. Don't make me. DON'T MAKE ME. NO! NO! NO! You're hurting me. Get away."

She starts to kick, shake her head, and writhe. "Get away. Get away. No. Don't make me." For a while she continues this way, her body becoming more and more tense, her outrage more pronounced. I imagine that she must be reexperiencing the incident from her childhood. Then suddenly her words indicate that we have slipped into another lifetime:

"They're raping me. They're raping me. Help! Help! HELP! There are six or seven of them. They're soldiers. I'm in a barn. My arms are tied. It's Russia somewhere. I'm a peasant girl about eleven or twelve. God, it's awful. They don't stop . . . I don't want to do this. I don't want to be here. LEAVE ME ALONE. I'm not going to feel this. I won't feel this. I won't show them anything."

Her pelvic area is stiff, her legs taut, her head turns from side to side. I urge her to let these parts of the body speak and express what is going on with them.

"I'm not going to feel this, I'll never show you I like it" (pelvis and genitals).

"Don't touch me! Get away! I'll kill you! I hate you. I hate you. I'll kick you! (legs).

"I'm not going to see this. It's not happening" (head).

For a while we work through this awful scene, and I encourage her to let her legs kick, to let her genitals record exactly what they feel, and to allow her head to see and understand all of it. There is kicking and weeping and rage and terrible confusion as for a while her genitals register both pleasure and pain. Gradually, as these sensations and movements surge through her body, she seems to experience a huge releasing and letting go of the earlier clenchings, all of which culminate in a bout of intense sobbing and convulsive movements in her pelvis.

Suddenly she is no longer with the soldiers:

"I'm in that garage. I don't want him to touch me. I don't want to do this. Don't make me. I just freeze up, but he doesn't hurt me. He's quite gentle, but my thighs just go rigid and I'm not really there."

I urge her to breathe deeply and see the similarity to the earlier rape scene.

"Oh, yes!" she says. "My body was remembering something else. It was like a flashback, a nightmare, but I didn't want to see it."

Follow Up

As Melinda surveys the two stories and gives herself permission to really see them now, she has all kinds of spontaneous recognitions: how just being touched always leads to a kind of freezing, how she is always somehow not present in sex, how she has always had fantasies of wanting to kick men, and so on. In a later session she reclaimed more of the Russian girl's story: how she had become pregnant, raised the child, a boy, alone, and had bitterly avoided contact with men from then onward, dying quite young from a wasting disease. The crucial events, however, were clearly locked into the rape scene at eleven or twelve. Her unconscious compulsion laid down in the previous life had led her—unconsciously, of course—to repeat a similar but far less violent sexual trauma in this life. The contemporary trauma served to reawaken the latent past life level of the complex, fraught as it was with terror, humiliation, and rage.

Case History #2

Cindy had been in therapy for quite a while, working on issues of deep emotional longing mixed with fear of rejection. She wanted dependable love so much, she said, that it was like "being eaten from inside," and she indicated her belly. She was also tormented by a severe childhood nightmare of flashing eyes and teeth in a dark corner of her childhood bedroom. In her interview the two issues seemed unrelated, but they were equally troubling to her. One well-meaning therapist had urged her to imagine a monster in the dark and then to befriend it, but somehow this ploy had not lessened the residual terror.

Working on the assumption that the childhood night of terror might well be a past-life flashback, I got her to find herself back in her bed as that terrified child:

"I'm standing in my bed, clinging to the railing. There are horrible yellow eyes in the corner and it looks like teeth. Mommy! Mommy! Please help me! They're trying to tear me up! Help me! Help me!"

Her mother comes and hugs her, saying, "It's only a dream, go back to sleep." She lies down, but still the eyes are there in the corner. Still the terror in her child's body—especially in her belly.

I direct her to look closely at the eyes and teeth and to stay with her feelings of terror, reminding her that her body as Cindy is safe and sound here in my office. I get her to repeat one phrase as she looks into the darkness:

"They're going to tear me up! They're going to tear me up! Oh, help! I'm running, I'm in a forest, it's almost dark. They're coming after me! I'm a boy, about six years old. They've caught me—it's a pack of wolfhounds! Help! HELP! Their teeth . . . ." (She screams and writhes violently.) "They're tearing me up . . . . Help me! Help me!"

After an agonizing five more minutes of screaming and writhing, Cindy suddenly goes completely limp.

"It's all over. I'm above the body. They (the wolfhounds) are all eating it. Ugh! They ripped out my guts, my neck, my chest. Oh, it's awful! But I'm dead now; I don't feel anything."

Cindy weeps for some time while I encourage her to breathe and let go of as much of the trauma as is possible, especially what is lodged in her belly. She realizes her belly is where she has always carried all the terror from this memory. I guide her to look back on the young boy's life until then. He had been the young son of a peasant woman who worked as a serving woman to a particularly brutal feudal lord. On a cruel impulse the lord and his cohorts had selected a human victim for their hunt one day and had driven the boy into the woods for sport. Although the mother had been helpless to prevent it, the boy felt deeply betrayed by her and by her master. The failure of Cindy's mother to rescue her from her night of terrors had unfortunately served only to reinforce an old deep wound of betrayal, a wound that had become increasingly generalized in adult life and had lodged itself symbolically in her stomach as a gnawing longing for trust and protection.

(From *Other Lives, Other Selves,*
a Jungian Therapist Discovers Past Lives—Doubleday)

X

Parent's Guide to Behavior Signs of Sexual Abuse

Statistics indicate that one out of four women and one out of eight adult men were sexually abused as children. This is a frightening statistic, and there is no indication that the odds are any better for our youngsters today. (Cited recently in the book *On the Outside Looking In* by President Reagan's son, Michael Reagan)

Sexual abuse is not always the parents' fault. Children can be abused when the parents are away, by brothers and sisters, neighbors, caretakers, or relatives.

Unless you as a parent happen to walk in on the incident in progress, it is extremely difficult to determine whether or not your child is being sexually abused. There have been cases in which a child has disclosed sexual abuse by an adult and then retracted the statement in court. Often they say that they made the original accusation in order to get back at the adult for some other reason. At that point there is no way to be certain which statement is true. Although, according to child sexual abuse expert Barbara Harrison, MSSW, the initial outcry statement is generally correct. In most cases, the child has been put under tremendous pressure not to tell and therefore will keep the secret as long as possible. So there is no easy way to be positive that sexual abuse is occurring.

The most important thing for the suspicious parent to do is to keep a balanced perspective; that is, do not over-react and do not under-react. Over-reaction can lead to false and damaging accusations and to guilt feelings on the child's part as well. Under-reaction, on the other hand, can lead to the "absent parent" syndrome, where the child feels abandoned and helpless. Above all, the child must know that he or she is believed.

According to Ms. Harrison, it is preferable to get the child to a therapist or child welfare worker ASAP and with no interrogation. The danger in "fishing for the truth" is that the legal system can later discount the child's testimony on the grounds that the parent has "put words into the child's mouth." Sometimes it is easier for a therapist who doesn't know the offender or parents personally to draw out the information, once it's clear there's a problem.

There are many signs of emotional disturbance in young children, some of which indicate chemical imbalances, drug abuse, innate personality disorders, or long-term reaction to childhood trauma (such as death of a loved-one, or witnessing a crime), and some indicate the possibility of sexual abuse, but these signs overlap. When parents observe an alarming number of "sexual abuse" signs of emotional disturbance appearing all at once, it is time to take action.

The following are symptoms that may indicate the possibility of some form of sexual abuse—from parent, brothers, sisters, neighbors, care-takers, or relatives:

Alcoholism and drug addiction
Self-mutilation: cutting, hitting, or burning
Obesity, compulsive overeating, anorexia, bulimia
Punishing attitude toward self and others
Battering others or signs of having been battered
Suicidal thoughts or behavior
Drastic revenge fantasies
Antisocial or extremely aggressive behavior
Outbursts of unreasonable, violent rage
Extreme hate or fear for a particular sex (male or female)
Repressed tears or screaming
Sections of time blocked out—lost days or years
Sliding or multiple personality, or sudden personality changes
Excessive jealousy or possessiveness
Attraction to abusive relationships

Intense dislike or mistrust of authority figures
Unusual knowledge or interest in sexual matters
Sexual acting-out in children and adolescents
Promiscuity or prostitition
Seductive dress and/or behavior
Extreme confusion and disorientation
Extreme or long-lasting depression
Feelings of hopelessness, despair
Feelings of self-contempt and loathing
Migraine headaches
Fainting or hyperactivity
Epilepsy seizures, with or without organic evidence
Frequent escapes into fantasy, often for long periods
"Seeing things" inside or outside the body or mind
"Voices" in the head or body
Nightmares and sleep disturbances
Claustrophobia and all other phobias
Fearful of any kind of doors, opened or closed
Mistrust of one's own reality
Difficulty in concentrating or listening
Learning disabilities
Bedwetting or fearful clinging to childhood securities, baby blankets, clothing, dolls, etc.
Running away from home
Terror of pelvic or rectal examinations
Damage to rectal, vaginal, or oral areas
Numbness in some areas of the skin, especially genitals
Stop in ovulation or genital development
Sexual dysfunction
Excessive fear of being touched
Compulsive bathing or scrubbing of genitals
Significant drop in grades or excessive overachieving at school
Emotional blunting, flatness of affect, or psychic numbing
Withdrawal from earlier activities and friends
Questions such as, "Is someone supposed to hurt kids?"

If you see these behavior signs in your young child or adolescent, ask questions; try to find out what is troubling them. If the symptoms persist, consult a mental health professional.

If abuse is confirmed, contact your local child protection agency; protect your child immediately from the suspected offender. Be a strong advocate and help your child with investigators; make sure he or she is interviewed by a specialist in child abuse. Be patient with the process and the length of time it takes for your child to make a full disclosure.

Get a medical exam for your child to protect against venereal disease and to gather possible evidence. However, do not become consumed with seeking vindication. For many children, telling their story and being believed promotes healing.

Next, have your child evaluated for therapy by a child-abuse specialist. Try to keep a calm environment at home and encourage a regular routine. Most of all, give them lots of love.

XI

Support Services Directory

As mentioned earlier, Alcoholics Anonymous and its successful twelve-step program has become the basis for many other programs that deal with addictive behavior. Each of these are nonprofit and free for the taking.

The following is not complete. New programs begin all the time, addressing nearly every issue imaginable. These are the ones I know about:

Adult Children of Alcoholics
Alateen
Al-Atot
Al-Anon
Alcoholics Anonymous
Bulimics/Anorexics Anonymous
Cocaine Anonymous
Co-dependents Anonymous
Co-dependents of Sex Addicts Anonymous
Child Abusers Anonymous
Debtors Anonymous
Emotions Anonymous
Fundamentalists Anonymous
Gamblers Anonymous
Narcotics Anonymous
Overeaters Anonymous

Parents Anonymous
Pills Anonymous
Sex Addicts Anonymous
Shoplifters Anonymous
Smokers Anonymous
Spenders Anonymous
Workaholics Anonymous

To find one of these groups in your area, look in the white pages of your telephone directory or call the Mental Health Association in the city near you. This is a wonderful resource and can guide you, not only to self-help groups, but also to the United Way Mental Health agencies whose sliding scales of fees are manageable for everyone.

The following is a list of some of the other support groups that may or may not be twelve-step programs:

AMI (Alliance for the Mentally Ill)
ANAD (Anorexia Nervosa and Associated Disorders)
COPED (Children of Parents with Emotional Disorders)
Depressive and Manic Depressive Association
Impotents Anonymous
Incest Survivors Anonymous
Loving Too Much
Parents Without Partners
SAFE (Self-Abuse Finally Ends)
Sibling Bond (Adult siblings of mentally ill individuals)
SOAR (Society of Agoraphobic Recovery)
Stepfamily Association
Survivors of Suicide
Tough Love

Appendix

Cathartic Writing

The following letter was written by a woman who swore she couldn't do it. I had to condense it because she wrote a record-breaking thirty-three pages. She was the youngest of seven children, all of whom were seriously abused by both parents, and her letter is a recollection of many incidents. Virginia was very eager for her letter to be published in this book because she was sure that she could never actually confront either of her parents. She had, in fact, tried to do that at one time, and her dad had told her she was crazy. For a while she believed him, and that's when she finally decided to see a therapist. She told me that the only way she had been able to get through the difficult task of writing the letter was to occasionally remind herself that God loves her.

Dear Mom,

I'm writing this letter for only one reason and I'm not sure I can actually ever mail it, but Dee Anna has asked me to do it so I'll try. *God loves me.*

Mom, I wonder if you even remember a time when I was about three years old and Jan (sis) was just a year older, and we were playing with your purse, while you were mopping the kitchen floor. We found some money in it and hid it out under the porch. When you found it missing you nearly went crazy. What happened next is somewhat distorted and fuzzy in my mind because it was so traumatic, but I remember you ducking my head in that filthy mop bucket over and over and over, and I was choking and crying and terrified. Then you did the same thing to Jan and then to me again, screeching that we were thieves. Jan ran out and got the money, and you finally stopped. I know that we were poor and you were frantic but I just don't see how any mother could do such a thing to her babies. I blocked that incident out of my memory for thirty years. When I recalled it I was left in such a state of depression that I almost gave up on living. *God loves me.*

Another memory that has come flooding back to me was when I was five and Jan was six and you and dad left us alone for a couple of days. The neighbors found out about it somehow and came and made us go home with them for the night and I remember hearing them talk about what they should do. They said something about child welfare and foster homes and I had no idea what was about to happen to us. I was so scared. I couldn't understand what all the "to-do" was about anyway, because this wasn't the first time we'd been left alone and you'd always come back before. But I thought maybe these people knew something that I didn't know and maybe you really wouldn't come home at all. Well, the next day you did come home and nothing more was said about child welfare or anything else. You never even explained where you'd been and you were really mad at the neighbors for interfering.

Mom, I know dad was abusive to you, especially when he was drunk. God, I remember one day when I was about thirteen, I came home and found blood spattered on the walls and floor and big blobs of hair all over the place. Of course, it wasn't the first time he'd beat on you but this time I thought he must have killed you. I was scared to death to go into the house but I thought you might be alive and need my help, so I did, and you came staggering out of your room. I gasped for air when I saw you. You looked like a monster with one eye swollen the size of a golf ball; your face and body bruised beyond recognition. You had bald spots on your head and it looked like you were bleeding tears of blood. I hated dad so much at that moment and I wondered if it was he who'd been killed. I hoped so, God help me.

I loved you so much, mom, and I know you were scared of dad too, but you never did anything to protect me. I can't believe that you didn't know he sexually abused all of us kids. My God, he did it right in front of you and you never did a thing to stop it. That time when he made me stand there while he showed me how a boy could *not* touch me. He stuck his nasty hand between my legs and on my breast and wouldn't let me move. Mom, you just *sat* there and never said a word. My face was burning with humiliation but I had to stand there

and let him manhandle me. When he finally finished his "demonstration" I went into the bedroom and sat in the dark. I wanted to die
from the degradation and the helplessness. I was fourteen years old.

That kind of stuff went on all my life, mom. Diane, (older sis) told
me just the other day that she had seen him lying naked on the bed
with me when I was eighteen months old or so with his penis in my
mouth. She said she ran in and told you and you put your hands
over your ears and said, "Don't tell me that!" Did you ever try to stop
him, mom? Please tell me that you did. *God loves me.*

If you're wondering why I'm writing to you instead of to dad, the
answer is, of course, that I've already done that a long time ago. It
took me a lot longer to recognize you as the "silent partner" in my
abusive treatment. Mom, I'm so damn mad at you now that I've
finally faced it that I don't think I can ever forgive you.

Do you want to know what the treatment I received in my childhood has done to my life? I'm sure you don't, but I'm going to tell
you anyway.

Dee Anna has asked me to recall the feelings I remember, and
what I realized is that I felt very dirty and very guilty not just as a
little girl, but for my whole life. I got married at fifteen just to get
away from home. In the eighteen years that have followed, I've been
addicted to alcohol, yes, just like dad, even though as a child I vowed
I would never touch the stuff. I've constantly struggled with abandonment issues, always afraid to love or care about anyone for fear
they might leave me. I've had so many extra-marital affairs that I'm
sure I couldn't even count them all. I have been depressed beyond
description and suicidal for years.

Through some incredible stroke of luck, or maybe because God
loves me, the boy I married eighteen years ago has stuck by me
through all the shit I have put him through and has supported me
enough to get me into the AA program and into therapy. It's taken
Dee Anna, my therapist, plus a psychiatrist who has me taking anti-
depressant medication just to help me get myself together. Mom,
when I started in therapy I really thought I was crazy. My four wonderful kids have miraculously survived all the years when I was act-
ing crazy, again because they were blessed with a daddy who over-
came my neglect. *God loves us all.*

I still struggle with old emotions and memories and at times the
emptiness is so strong it feels as though a hole has been bored

through my soul. But I now know more peace than I have in all of my thirty-three years. *God loves me.*

Virginia

Virginia has reconsidered the idea of confronting her parents. The work she did in therapy, especially the writing, seemed to give her courage. She approached her mother about the mop bucket incident expecting her to deny it. She did not, but tried to justify it saying that she was so desperate for money and so consumed with worry that she simply reacted as she did because the girls were so sneaky. She did not seem to comprehend that putting a child's head under water was inappropriate, no matter *how* badly they misbehaved. She dismissed the sexual abuse by saying, "That's just the way your daddy showed that he loved you."

Virginia gave up at that point but did not feel that the confrontation was a failure. After all, the purpose was to say the things she needed to say, not to get confirmation.

This woman did her writing in a very unique way. It's almost a poem, and, I think, very moving. She claims to feel no anger for her parents, only *nothing.*

I hate the cold, harsh, emotionally sterile environment you provided for my childhood. But for you, I feel nothing.

I hate the way you always made me feel such deep shame, Mom, for the least little thing. But for you I feel nothing.

I hate it that you never wanted to tell the people you worked with that you were a grandmother. But for you I feel nothing.

I hate it that you offered money for an abortion but no emotional support for my pregnancy. But for you I feel nothing.

I hate the way you always expected some terrible tragedy just around the corner. But for you I feel nothing.

Mom, I hate the way you treat Dad like a baby, and Dad, I hate how you allow her to do that. But for you I feel nothing.

I hate that I have no memories of ever being hugged or kissed or told "I love you." But for you I feel nothing.

I hate the status of second class family member I was given because I was a girl. But for you I feel nothing.

I hate your complete inability to experience any kind of spiritual or emotional growth. But for you I feel nothing.

I hate that I have to hide the true "me" behind the "me" you want me to see. But for you I feel nothing.

And when you die, I will hate the hassle of having to plan a funeral and close out an estate. But for you, I'll feel nothing.

There is probably as much seething anger, passive-aggressive anger, in this piece of writing as I have ever heard from an individual. Bless her heart, she has her work cut out for her in getting to it.

This little poem was written by my good friend Dr. Fred Fisher, who is himself an adult survivor:

Justice

Survivors seldom find success,
In getting parents to confess.
Abusers seem to take delight,
In a pose of always being right.

One wonders when the tables turn;
In fact, do parents ever learn?
Methinks it happens as they die,
When they get found out in their lie.

Suggested Readings

Bloomfield, H. *Making Peace With Your Parents*. Del Mar, California: Bloomfield Productions, 1983.

Bradshaw, J. *The Family*. Deerfield Beach, Fl.: Health Communications, Inc., 1988.

Bradshaw, J. *Healing The Shame That Binds You*. Deerfield Beach, Fl.: Health Communications, Inc., 1988.

Erickson, E. H. *Childhood and Society*. New York: W. W. Norton and Company, 1963.

Forward, S. *Toxic Parent*. New York, Bantam, 1989.

Gill, Eliana. *Outgrowing the Pain*. San Francisco: Launch Press, 1983.

Halpern, H. *How To Break Your Addiction To a Person*. New York: McGraw-Hill Book Company, 1982.

Leonard, L.S. *Healing The Father-Daughter Relationship*. Boulder: Shambhala, 1985.

Lifton, R. *The Broken Connection*. New York: Simon and Schuster, 1979.

Miller, A. *The Drama of the Gifted Child*. New York: Basic Books, Inc., 1981.

Norwood, R. *Women Who Love Too Much*. New York: Simon and Schuster, 1985.

Reagan, M. *On The Outside Looking In*. New York: Zebra Books, 1989.

Silver, L. *The Misunderstood Child*. New York: McGraw-Hill Book Company, 1984.

Wilson, J. "Conflict, Stress and Growth." *Strangers at Home*. Edited by Charles R. Figley. New York: Praeger Press, 1980.

Woititz, J. *Adult Children of Alcoholics*. Pompano Beach: Health Communication, 1983.

Yalom, I. *The Theory and Practice of Group Psychotherapy*. New York: Harper and Row Publishers, 1975.

The Adult Survivor is a newsletter now published bimonthly (six times a year) in a four page format. Each issue includes letters, professional input, and survivor opinion. We invite you to join us!

The Adult Survivor is devoted to adults who were victimized by child abuse and is published bimonthly. You can support this endeavor by subscribing at a cost of $8 per year.

> The Adult Survivor
> 1318 Ridgecrest Circle
> Denton, Texas 76205

Enclosed is my check (or money order) for $ _____.
Please begin my subscription immediately.

Name _____

Address _____

_____

Please send us the names and addresses of others who might be interested.

Other titles by Station Hill Press

PERCEPTION

The Reality Illusion: How You Make the World You Experience, Ralph Strauch, $10.95 paper.

TOUCH THERAPY

Where Healing Waters Meet: Touching Mind and Emotion Through the Body, Dr. Clyde Ford, Foreword by Marilyn Ferguson, $19.95 cloth.

Job's Body: A Handbook for Bodywork, Deane Juhan, Foreword by Ken Dychtwald, $29.95 cloth.

PSYCHOLOGY/ENERGETICS

Emotional First Aid: A Crisis Handbook, Sean Haldane, $9.95 paper.

Music and Sound in the Healing Arts: An Energy Approach, John Beaulieu, $11.95 paper, $19.95 cloth.

The Lover Within: Opening to Energy in Sexual Practice, Julie Henderson, $9.95 paper.

The Shaman's Doorway: Opening Imagination to Power and Myth, Stephen Larsen, $10.95 paper.

Dragon Rises, Red Bird Flies: Psychology and Chinese Medicine, Leon Hammer, M.D., Foreword by Ted Kaptchuk, $28.95 cloth.

MEDITATION

Self-Liberation Through Seeing With Naked Awareness: An Introduction to the Nature of One's Own Mind in the Tibetan Dzogchen Tradition, Translated with Commentary by John Reynolds, Foreword by Namkhai Norbu, $14.95 paper, $29.95 cloth.

The Cycle of Day and Night: An Essential Tibetan Text on the Practice of Contemplation, Namkhai Norbu, translated and edited by John Reynolds, $10.95 paper.

SELF-HEALING

Lupus Novice: Towards Self-Healing, Laura Chester, $10.95 paper,$16.95 cloth.

COMMUNICATION

The Phone Book: Breakthrough Phone Skills for Fun, Profit and Enlightenment, Richard Zarro and Peter Blum, $9.95 paper.

CHILDREN'S EDUCATION

Childmade: Awakening Children to Creative Writing, Cynde Gregory, $10.95 paper, $19.95 cloth.

Available in local bookstores or order direct from:

Station Hill Press
Barrytown, New York 12507

Emotional First Aid
A Crisis Handbook
Sean Haldane

Coping with grief, anger, fear, joy and parent/child conflicts.

In his book *Emotional First Aid*, Dr. Haldane has provided his readers with practical information that will serve them well in most of the inter-personal and intra-personal crises they may encounter.

> DR. STANLEY KRIPPNER
> Saybrook Institute

Haldane's clarity in the face of extreme anger, joy, grief, and fear is as useful for therapists, conference organizers, and parents as it is for poets–anyone interested in the precise details of human expression. He teaches us, quickly and responsibly, how to give appropriate assistance in those times when emotion becomes unbearable. His attitude is the one I want to reach for in an emergency.

> NOR HALL
> author of *The Moon and The Virgin*

In this fine book, Haldane has for the first time set out clearly and accessibly for everyone the basic means to ease a difficult emotional passage and made clear, as well, the difference between this skillful immediate aid and the deeper work that is to require therapy.

> JULIE HENDERSON
> author of *The Lover Within*

Emotional First Aid is the first book to address immediate emotional crisis as distinct from therapy and mental health in general. It deals with grief, anger, fear, joy, and also the complex feelings of parent/child conflicts–all emotions that can lead to further withdrawal, illness, or even violence. Extraordinarily well written, this is the first book to draw on Reichian character analysis to explain how differences in individuals and in specific emotions call for very different kinds of responses if one is to lend support without invasion. Just as efficient physical first aid can prevent extended medical treatment, immediate emotional first aid may precede therapy or even preclude it. Haldane's approach and language are straight forward and clear; his book will help any reader face the ups and downs of emotional life. Rich in detail it will serve the layman as well as the professional counselor.

Sean Haldane is a psychotherapist noted for his workshops in crisis and marital therapy and for his books on literature and psychological theory, including Couple Dynamics: A Guide to Sexual/Emotional Enhancement *and* Applied Reichian Therapy. *He graduated from Oxford University and the Saybrook Institute, and now lives in Halifax, Nova Scotia.*

A Crisis Handbook

EMOTIONAL

FIRST AID

coping with

GRIEF·ANGER·FEAR·JOY

PARENT/CHILD CONFLICTS

Sean Haldane

$9.95 paper, ISBN 0-88268-071-4
160 pages, 6x9
bibliography, index
PSYCHOLOGY, HEALTH, CRISIS
INTERVENTION

Where Healing Waters Meet
Touching Mind and Emotion Through the Body
Dr. Clyde W. Ford
Foreword by Marilyn Ferguson

A "language of touch" to heal body, mind, and spirit.

Clyde Ford's impressive clinical work demonstrates that the body and the mind do not merely interact, but are rather one and the same.... Rich in case studies, theory and useful techniques, this book is a source of inspiration.
DEANE JUHAN
author of *Job's Body: A Handbook for Bodywork*

An excellent book which should be read by all therapists, especially those who use touch and similar techniques to get in touch with the deeper issues of a person's problems whether they are physical, psychological, or spiritual.
ELIZABETH KUBLER-ROSS
author of *On Death and Dying*

The oneness of Body-Mind and its all-embracing relation to the sense of touch is clearly and impressively presented.
LAURA HUXLEY
author of *The Child of Your Dreams*

Dr. Ford's book is an important step in rediscovering the body, and the mind and spirit beyond it. It will be a great help for many in opening the domain that is spiritual and transpersonal.
LARRY DOSSEY M.D.
author of *Space, Time and Medicine*

While touching a patient during a routine physical examination, the author, a chiropractor, unintentionally evoked in the woman a forgotten memory of incest experienced 25 years earlier. Thus was born somatosynthesis, a unique process of healing that brings psychological and spiritual therapies together with the principles of therapeutic touch. A wealth of case studies illustrates how Dr. Ford has used this dramatic therapy, based on touch rather than talk, to ease physical and emotional pain and to help his patients find meaning and purpose in their lives. He also shows the reader how to create "body maps" relating specific areas of the body to emotional, psychological, and spiritual issues. Healing professionals who work with touch-based methods of therapy will find the book a rich source of ideas and techniques; general readers will find it simply inspirational.

Dr. Clyde W. Ford has a private chiropractic practice in Richmond, Virginia. The past president of the Foundation for the Advancement of Chiropractic Research, he has written and lectured widely on alternative healing, and recently established ISTAR, the Institute for Somatosynthesis Training and Research.

$19.95 cloth, ISBN 0-88268-080-3
260 pages, 6x9
notes, bibliography, index
MIND, BODY, SPIRIT, PSYCHOLOGY

The Swimming Dragon
A Chinese Way to Fitness, Beautiful Skin, Weight Loss & High Energy

Dr. T. K. Shih

Guidance for weight loss, beauty, and high energy.

One of the simplest Chinese exercises passed on from ancient times, the Swimming Dragon uniquely stimulates health, improves muscle tone, and creates beautiful skin while balancing energy and metabolism to control weight. People of all ages and abilities can master the graceful, serpentine movements easily. With 15 minutes a day, this form improves posture, relaxes the body, increases flexibility in the joints and muscles, and calms the mind as it exercises and brings healing energy to the vital internal organs. It reaches all of the muscles, including deep muscles close to the bones that are not reached by normal exercise. The book is straightforward and detailed with numerous photographs showing every aspect of the practice. In addition to increasing energy, improving breathing, and contributing to general fitness, the exercise induces a meditative state of peacefulness and well-being. And it constitutes a complete art of life-extension.

The unique Chinese exercise for weight loss

the swimming dragon

A Chinese Way to Fitness, Beautiful Skin, Weight Loss & High Energy

T. K. Shih

Tzu Kuo Shih is a fifth generation healer born in Shanghai and the first to teach the Swimming Dragon in the West. Noted in China as a ch'i kung master, doctor, cancer specialist, as well as a painter and author, he currently teaches t'ai chi and ch'i kung in Manhattan, Woodstock, and Kingston, New York, and lectures throughout the U.S.

$9.95 paper, ISBN 0-88268-063-3
120 pages, 6 1/2 x 9 1/4
over 50 photos and drawings
HEALTH, EXERCISE, SPIRITUAL PRACTICE

VIDEO/VHS
Master Tzu Kuo Shih teaches Swimming Dragon Form on videocassette.
Catalog cost $29.95, regularly $49.95

Childmade
Awakening Children to Creative Writing
Cynde Gregory

Bring out the writer in every child

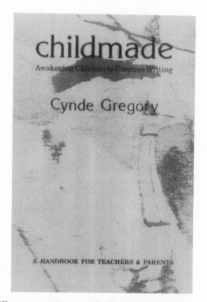

This is a lively and compassionate guide. The author knows what she's writing about.
> **NATALIE GOLDBERG**
> author of *Writing Down the Bones*

A lively mind and a concern for children are at work here. The potential for expanding creative possibilities at an earlier age ought to spark the interest of educators in many fields.
> **HELEN REGUEIRO ELAM**
> author of *The Limits of Imagination*

A young woman of extreme literary integrity and devotion.
> **WILLIAM KENNEDY**
> author of *Ironweed*

Childmade should be read immediately by every teacher of writing.
> **DR. EUGENE GARBER**
> Department of English, SUNY Albany

My students created the most detailed, imaginative and exciting poetry. It was as if she opened up a dam of creativity that flowed from each child into their poetry.
> **RON FRIEDMAN**
> third grade teacher

After twelve years of classroom experience with over 10,000 elementary school children, Cynde Gregory offers this comprehensive guide to the joys and skills of developing creative writing in children. *Childmade* provides the tools to stimulate children's subconscious imaginations and help them channel their visions into poems and stories. At the heart of the book is a unique meditation technique designed to fill young writers with detailed visions out of which writing will easily grow. Enlivened with charming examples of children's writing, the book speaks to parents, teachers, homeschoolers, and writers, featuring practical advice, serious literary discussion, and dozens of specific writing projects.

Cynde Gregory has taught creative writing in public and private schools throughout New York State. A resident of Woodstock, New York, her poetry and fiction have appeared in numerous journals.

$10.95 paper, ISBN 0-88268-088-9
$19.95 cloth, ISBN 0-88268-093-5
256 pages, 6 x 9
line drawings, index, bibliography
EDUCATION